Massey College Lectures 1974-75

Beyond industrial growth

Edited by

ABRAHAM ROTSTEIN

Preface by

ROBERTSON DAVIES

Master, Massey College

University of Toronto Press

Toronto and Buffalo

Library of Congress Cataloging in Publication Data
Main entry under title:

Beyond industrial growth.

Lectures given at Massey College, University of Toronto, 1974-1975.
1. Canada – Economic conditions – 1945- – Addresses, essays, lectures.
2. Canada – Economic policy – Addresses, essays, lectures.   3. Natural resources
– Canada – Addresses, essays, lectures.
I. Rotstein, Abraham. II. Massey College.
HC115.B45   338'.0971   76-7440
ISBN 0-8020-2228-6
ISBN 0-8020-6286-5 pbk.

Preface

Massey College considered itself privileged to have presented the series of lectures which were called 'Beyond Industrial Growth' during the academic year 1974-75, for two reasons: they allowed six distinguished men to offer their opinions on a theme of pressing importance to the Western world at the present time; they involved the College in a kind of political discussion especially suited to an academic institution because it was not of narrow import or partisan significance.

Universities cannot and should not involve themselves in short-term political concerns, but as custodians of intellectual liberty and cultural advance they cannot sequester themselves from public affairs. The theme of these lectures, so different in approach and conclusions, is one of inescapable significance for our time. The College was a proper place to air this theme and thereby provoke further discussion and, perhaps, some action.

We could not offer them to large audiences at first hearing, but thanks to the interest of the Canadian Broadcasting Corporation the lectures have been made available to a national audience, and their preservation on tape ensures that they will reach audiences still to come. The publication of the book you now hold is another step toward making this remarkable series available to students and concerned people everywhere.

On behalf of Massey College, I repeat here the thanks already expressed to the Walter and Duncan Gordon Foundation for their generosity in making the lectures possible. It has been a distinguished instance of private patronage. The College is also most grateful to Professor Abraham Rotstein, who undertook the considerable task of organizing the lectures and of seeing this book through the press.

Robertson Davies
June 1975
Master, Massey College

Contents

Introduction

Since the coming of the Industrial Revolution, we have assumed that social progress must be borne on the wings of technology. For about two centuries we have knitted ever more closely our relations with the machine, moved by a faith in the unfolding of a benign destiny.

From the first, both warnings and utopian visions came in literary and political imagery. Mary Shelley sensed the looming Frankenstein in 1810. Others such as Fourier, Saint-Simon, and Robert Owen sensed that a perfection in human institutions was dawning. This interplay of apocalypse and utopia was the counterpoint of the machine in the human imagination. It is not surprising that strands of both persist throughout the new debate – the debate on the end of industrial growth. Whatever impetus both apocalypse and utopia add to the discussion, the central issues themselves must now be confronted.

When the opportunity to present a lecture series was offered to Massey College by the Walter and Duncan Gordon Foundation, we wrote to our prospective lecturers as follows:

'The central theme of this lecture series is of great importance and has increasingly captured the imagination of thoughtful people throughout the Western world. I refer specifically to the broad discussion initiated by the Club of Rome on the limits to industrial growth. There are many large issues involved here, including the growth of population, the indiscriminate proliferation of technology and the contamination of the environment, the projected shortages of certain raw materials by the turn of the century, and so on.

'These issues individually have now become the subject of much public debate and some valid objections have in fact been raised about the analytical techniques used by the Club of Rome. Nevertheless a central concern is now coming into focus and remains the starting point of our own lecture series: How are we to orient our thinking and our preparations for a society that is not committed to economic growth as its first priority? How are we to conceive of the political, economic and cultural stresses and strains that will accompany a transition to 'the steady state' by the turn of the century? Put differently, how will we re-define social progress in other than the conventional economic and technical terms?

'Six eminent Canadians are being invited to take up this theme from their own particular vantage point free of any restriction or direction other than the broad framework we have postulated above. We expect however, that their lectures will relate in some way to the Canadian situation and to some of its particular challenges and opportunities.

'Our intention is to avoid contributions that are highly specialized or technical. We believe that the formulation of such an alternative focus for Canadian society should be done in a broad way, accessible to the intelligent general public. We also hope to bypass rigid or dogmatic positions particularly those of a traditional or sentimental bent. The entire venture can be regarded as a forward-looking exercise in the Canadian social imagination.'

It would be gratifying to discover, among the threads that run through the diverse viewpoints of these lectures, something of a Canadian sensibility. But this is not immediately apparent. Disagreement on the findings and implications of the first report of the Club of Rome is as rife in this country as it is elsewhere. What we can discern in common perhaps is a modulated sensibility – a disavowal equally of an apocalyptic outlook as well as of a dogmatic utopianism. Some-where in the middle range, an assessment is made of the increasing constraints on industrial growth as a way of life, as well as an assessment of the human and political resources and traditions we may bring to bear in the present situation.

Senator Lamontagne from his long experience and interest in this issue intro-duces the problem. He reminds us of the 'steady state' in the centuries prior to the industrial revolution and thus of the exceptional nature of the path of indus-trial growth on which we embarked at that time.

In a country presumably as rich in resources as Canada, we discover some dis-concerting facts. Despite our vast area, most of our arable land is already under cultivation, but is rapidly being taken out of agricultural production by growing urban and industrial use. Energy supply poses a similar problem. It is substantially scarcer and more expensive to develop from both fossil fuel and hydro-electric sources. In turn, the age of 'easy ore' is over for Canadian mining. At present exponential rates of production, reserves in Canada of key minerals such as cop-per, nickel, lead, and zinc will last between 14 and 31 years; asbestos and potash, 36 and 38 years respectively; and iron ore 94 years. Even our pulp and paper supply will be constrained by the 1990s.

One of Senator Lamontagne's most important conclusions is that 'the private and public institutions which launched the exponential era are no longer adequate to face the problems of that period and to bring mankind into another steady state.' He is particularly concerned with the paralysis of the collective decision-making process when confronted with the task of massive transformation. Senator Lamontagne offers a practical proposal for a Canadian Centre for Futures Studies as a form of 'anticipatory democracy' to develop a future-oriented national consensus.

The three essays that follow pursue in greater detail the political, economic, and social issues involved in institutional transformation. The authors are A.W. Johnson, Charles Taylor, and Claude Castonguay.

Al Johnson focuses on the outmoded framework with which we have tended to view the economy when seeing it exclusively in the commercial market model. Most of the issues – global as well as domestic – that arise are increasingly in the public sector and require a different mode of decision-making from that derived from the traditional supply-demand-price mechanism. In particular, there is a wider range of values which come into play, from compassion to egalitarianism, and they demand a new framework for resource allocation other than the usual notions of efficiency and profitability. This is not a matter of replacing a 'rational' approach with an 'irrational' one but, on the contrary, of becoming more deliberate and direct in regard to our social aims and responsibilities. We must abandon the pretence that these problems can be handled by a pseudo-commercial approach. Economics, in short, must widen its horizons to encompass political and social issues if it is to remain useful in the new circumstances.

The stark issue in the political realm is whether we can accomplish the needed transition while retaining democratic institutions. The alternative prospect is a highly authoritarian regime. Professor Taylor points to the path of egalitarianism as the only acceptable mode to produce democratic consensus. A consumption standard equivalent to a normal decent life would need to be available to the most disadvantaged in our society to avoid a final and decisive conflict among the various economic groups.

Claude Castonguay has several reservations about the premises and conclusions of the Club of Rome's report. But he sees very clearly the need to transcend the overriding compulsion toward economic growth. He faces the issues of creating a more human environment on a broad front: in our social welfare programs, in our cities, and – most of all – in our places of work. He advocates a path of reform whose hallmark is democratic participation by citizens on the various levels of decision-making that affect their lives. Most challenging is the search for a new philosophy of work requiring a subordination of existing authoritarian management practices towards a fuller involvement of the work force in production decisions. Admittedly, there are costs of such a process in terms of economic efficiency, but an industrial society can afford to be free and democratic in every sphere.

Both Charles Taylor and Claude Castonguay underline and explore the implications of Canadian federalism in the new circumstances we are considering. For Taylor it is an occasion to reap the benefits of greater decentralization to avert more authoritarian political structures. For Castonguay, it becomes an occasion for Quebec legitimately to demarcate and govern in its own areas of responsibility in recognition of the authentic nature of the two societies of which Canada is composed.

In the final two essays Vivian Rakoff and George Grant offer divergent explorations of human resilience under the stress that may come. Vivian Rakoff offers his own testimony to the human continuity that lies at the base of seemingly random and oppressive social change. It is a reassurance that we have, within our social memory, some long-standing human resources to meet the future.

George Grant recognizes that the resolution of the dilemmas of the steady state may take an even greater mastery of human nature than it took to create industrial growth. At issue is the 'darkness' that technique and the machine society have brought into our inner lives in a way which can barely be discerned. Grant evokes a pristine memory of what came before, so that we can begin to see 'beyond.'

We expect that the debate on industrial growth in this country as elsewhere will gather momentum over the next few years. The early evidence of malfunction on immediate issues such as inflation, the world monetary system, and the depletion of our oil and gas resources will necessarily force a larger reappraisal of the major premises to which our society clings. The impetus to change will result from a convergence of issues on different levels. But no progress is possible unless we develop a wider framework to govern the directions in which we will move.

I should like to acknowledge the splendid co-operation throughout this project of Mrs Bette Hooper, secretary of our lecture series and Mr Colin Friesen, the indefatigable bursar of Massey College.

Professor A.G. Falconer of University College translated Claude Castonguay's paper into English.

Professor Douglas LePan, a Senior Fellow of this College, played a central role in the planning and formulation of this project.

The superior editorial judgement and unfailing good humour of Mr. R.I.K. Davidson of the University of Toronto Press is also greatly appreciated.

Abraham Rotstein
Senior Fellow, Massey College

Steadying the unsteady state

MAURICE LAMONTAGNE

The loss of the steady state

When Denis Meadows and his team published the first report to the Club of Rome in 1972,[1] modern societies were so addicted to growth that *The Limits to Growth* caught them completely by surprise. Many critics dismissed it as doomsday prophecy,[2] but in its substance it contained nothing not already known.

Physical scientists are long used to describing the earth and its environment as a balanced system. Biologists have developed the concept of the organic growth of living systems; Raymond Pearl showed in 1925 that such growth followed an S-shaped or sigmoid curve, eventually reaching saturation.[3] In 1929 Donald Foster, a geologist, observed that mining districts evolve during their history through successive states analogous to those of infancy, adolescence, maturity, and old age. King Hubert, who knows as much about fossil fuel exploration as anyone alive, showed in 1956 that the rate of production of any exhaustible resource went through a symmetrical cycle and that the peak in the US crude oil production would be reached around 1970.[4]

Classical economists described the behaviour of the economy as a constant search for equilibrium. John Stuart Mill asserted in his *Principles of Political Economy* that the stationary state was needed because 'the increase in wealth is not boundless ... and population must be contained and balanced to enable mankind to obtain, in the greatest degree, all the advantage of both cooperation and social intercourse.' Marx saw the advent of communism as a steady state and the final stage of an evolution that began with feudalism and continued with capitalism and dictatorial socialism. Schumpeter envisaged a circular flow resulting from the vanishing of the entrepreneur and the rise of socialism. Lord Keynes stated in 1930 that economic growth would stop 'gradually, not as a catastrophe ... (as) there will be ever larger and larger classes and groups of people from whom problems of economic necessity have been practically removed.'[5] W.W. Rostow, in *The Stages of Economic Growth*, contended that 'some sixty years after take-off, what may be called maturity is generally attained' and that at the post-maturity stage, 'through the political process, Western societies have chosen to allocate increased resources to social welfare and security.'[6]

Thus the concept of the steady state has a long history in various scientific disciplines. Yet, just as mankind is beginning to suffer from the pains of undifferentiated quantitative growth and of an open-ended system perhaps for the first time in its history, *The Limits to Growth* caused a scandal. It is much rather the prediction of the so-called optimists that cancerous growth can go on almost indefinitely which should be questioned and challenged as an invalid proposition encouraging dangerous complacency. Indeed, according to King Hubert, the present phase of exponential growth 'represents but a brief transitional epoch between two very much longer periods each characterized by rates of change so slow as to be regarded essentially as a period of non-growth.'[7]

In the current debate, those who forecast the end of the exponential era are the realists. Their view is based on the history of past civilizations, on the fact that our universe is finite, and on a concept which has scientific validity. We should be wary of over-optimism. In the Greek legend, Prometheus said, 'I caused mortals to cease foreseeing doom ... I placed in them blind hopes.' We should refuse any such dangerous gift; blind hopes inevitably lead to doom.

The history of quantitative growth, at least since the decline of the Roman Empire, can be divided roughly into two major periods. The first lasted until the end of the eighteenth century and corresponded largely to the steady state. It produced growth processes and trends which were more or less in balance; it reflected an arithmetic progression. With the Industrial Revolution and other concomitant major innovations in medicine, agriculture, and transportation, mankind, especially in the West, experienced a major turning point in the first part of the nineteenth century. The second period, the exponential era, really began after 1850. It produced explosive and unbalanced growth processes which, in spite of their dissimilarities, their rising and declining trends, generally reflected a geometric progression.

Throughout this history, man showed a remarkable ability to adjust to and even to reinforce prevailing basic patterns. During the first period, he developed attitudes and institutions which helped consolidate the steady state and the closed system. As the second period gained momentum, he manifested new aspirations and created new social systems which contributed to the acceleration of exponential growth and the development of an open-ended world.

As we reach the last quarter of the twentieth century, many signs indicate the emergence of a second major turning point in modern times. We are beginning to realize that exponential growth, in its physical parameters, cannot go on forever. We also have the feeling that there are human limits to growth. Gunther S. Stent sees a change in the social ethos and 'in progress an element of negative feedback.'[8] Rising expectations, still shared by the majority, lead to confrontation and turmoil in the world and within nations. The lack of consensus paralyses the collective decision-making process. The institutions which provided the basis for the exponential era are weakened. The 'horizontal society' has replaced the 'vertical society' but it has produced a 'random society.'

Mankind is reaching a crossroads of social decision. If we continue to pursue indiscriminate growth, we will sooner, rather than later, face what John Platt has called a 'storm of crisis problems' and a substantial decline in the quality of life. On the other hand, while the new social ethos and the negative feedback of 'progress' may contribute to ease the situation, it is unrealistic to expect that the transition from exponential to constant growth will be accomplished in time to avoid the storm that will come by natural instinct or a sort of collective indigestion. If the transition is to be made smoothly, it can only take place by conscious choice, calculation, and planning. The second report to the Club of Rome, *Mankind at the Turning Point*,[9] claims that the world has about fifty years to make this adjustment, provided that action begins now. Will we be able to develop quickly new goals, new institutions, and new processes which will enable us to cope effectively with this tremendous challenge and to build the basis for a new humanistic steady state during the next fifty years?

That is the question.

THE ERA OF THE STEADY STATE

The first eighteen centuries of the Christian era were marked by substantial achievements both in terms of quantitative and qualitative growth. However, the stock of capital and people increased slowly enough until the end of the eighteenth century to correspond approximately to the conditions of the steady state.

Technological progress was slow. The hygienic conditions and the medical knowledge developed by the Greeks and the Romans did not substantially improve until 1775. Technical know-how in other areas also remained about the same. The traditional sources of energy continued to prevail until the development of the steam engine. The compass was a great invention, but the speed of transportation did not increase significantly until the first part of the nineteenth century with the steamboat and the railways. Printing was another major achievement but the great revolution in communications began only around 1850 with the telegraph. Farming methods began to improve after 1770.

Living conditions remained remarkably stable at low levels. Jean Fourastié has estimated that during the eighteenth century more than 85 per cent of the typical family budget in France had to be devoted to food, mainly to the consumption of bread.[10] The birth rate was high, but so was the death rate. In 1800, life expectancy was still about the same as it had been in Ancient Rome. As a result, world population grew very slowly; even at the end of the period, it doubled in 250 years, from 1600 to 1850.[11] In other words, during the first eighteen centuries of the Christian era, the technological frontier expanded steadily but slowly. The 'limits to growth' were rather narrow boundaries determined by the whims of nature, acute epidemics and famines, and the low innovative potential of man who had not yet learned to dominate his environment.

The steady state of this technological and demographic infrastructure was reinforced by a vertical society with static institutions. The majority of the population was poor, uneducated, fatalistic, and passive. It interpreted its condition as the result of a natural order of divine origin. The leaders, even great thinkers like Pascal, were careful not to destroy this belief. Religion gave meaning to poverty. Decisions were autocratic but unquestioned.

The main populated areas of the world were living in isolation, but their quantitative growth and their social institutions followed more or less the same patterns. The technological gap with all its consequences had not yet developed. The steady state and its narrow growth potential represented not only a national but a universal order.

THE EXPONENTIAL ERA

Toward the beginning of the nineteenth century, a period of rapid technological change emerged, particularly in Europe and North America. The first part of that century can be seen as a transition between the steady state and exponential growth. Around 1850 a number of Western countries went through the stage of their industrial 'take-off,' a series of important innovations introduced earlier was diffused more widely, the exponential era was launched.

The first major technological revolution has been described as the Industrial Revolution. While it is true that the steam engine and its numerous applications, together with the blast furnace and other important innovations, led to a fundamental transformation of industry, the new revolution was much wider in scope: it extended also to transportation, agriculture, communications, and medicine.

At the end of the nineteenth century another major technological revolution appeared. It was characterized by electricity and such products as petroleum, natural gas, hydraulic power, motor cars, tractors, aeroplanes, telephones, films, radio and later television, paper using wood as a raw material, substitutes for steel, a whole range of electrical goods and chemical products which had a great impact on agriculture and medicine. These new technologies were diffused after the First World War and more rapidly after the Second.

In the late 1950s, a third major technological revolution appeared. Its most spectacular achievements are illustrated by commercial nuclear energy inaugurated in 1956, the launching of the first Sputnik in 1957, the solid-state computer in 1958, the transistor, plastics and 'artificial' products, the Green Revolution, the laser, biological engineering, and a whole range of new drugs.

These illustrations indicate that if the progress experienced since the late 1950s were to stop today, the full consequences of the utilization and diffusion of inventions already made would be far-reaching and all-embracing. However, the new revolution has become a continuing process supported by a systematic and massive research and development effort. This is its unique feature.

Thus the Industrial Revolution inaugurated a major turning point for mankind. Man really began to understand and to dominate his environment. At first, the true nature and the expansionist character of the changes were not readily apparent. The planet's potential was still relatively untouched and there was plenty of room for manoeuvre. Since man was just beginning to learn how to master nature, he did not realize that he was becoming a sorcerer's apprentice; he could not conceive that he was starting a flood of knowledge which would be difficult to stop.

As the successive technological revolutions provided the infrastructure required to launch the exponential era, their cumulative impact was reinforced by man's rising expectations and by other major innovations which replaced or weakened the social institutions and processes of the steady state. While the old attitudes, techniques, and institutions had worked together to limit quantitative growth and to provide a slow-moving equilibrium, the new forces were all leading toward unlimited growth and rapid change.

As the average citizen perceived the new potentialities, he lost his old fatalism and his belief in the old natural order. He developed almost unlimited aspirations and an acquisitive spirit. A little-known author named William Foster Lloyd described this new 'rational' man in 1833. Garret Hardin has summarized Lloyd's scenario in a recent article entitled 'The Tragedy of the Commons':

'Picture a pasture open to all ... As a rational being each herdsman seeks to maximize his gain. Explicitly or implicitly, more or less consciously, he asks: 'What is the utility to me of adding one more animal to my herd?' This utility has two components:
1 A positive component, which is a function of the increment of one animal. Since the herdsman receives all the proceeds from the sale of the additional animal, the positive utility is nearly *plus* 1.

2 A negative component which is the function of the additional overgrazing created by one more animal. But since the effects of overgrazing are shared by all the herdsmen, the negative utility for any particular decision-making herdsman is only a fraction of *minus* 1.

'Adding together the component partial utilities, the rational herdsman concludes that the only sensible course for him to pursue is to add another animal to his herd. And another; and another. But this is the conclusion reached by each and every rational herdsman sharing a commons. Therein is the tragedy. Each man is locked in to a system that compels him to increase his herd without limit – in a world that is limited.'[12]

The new rational man was a powerful force in the launching of the exponential era. In addition, a series of social innovations diffused mainly after 1800 also contributed greatly to the exponential explosion. Methods of industrial production were drastically changed, leading to the factory system, mass production, and improved productivity. The structure of the firm changed from individual ownership and partnerships to the limited liability company and the gigantic modern corporation. Capitalism replaced feudalism and, contrary to Marx' forecast, socialism developed as an alternative path to growth, as a competitor of capitalism instead of its successor, thus giving rise to two competing imperalisms.

Universities gradually ceased to be sanctuaries of pure knowledge and started to adjust to the new industrialism. Education became more easily accessible, since new skills were required, and thus was a powerful solvent of the traditional social stratification. As the belief in the old static order weakened, the power of the Church declined. Rising expectations led to a greater collective involvement in the decision-making process: the rise of democracy meant the decline of absolute monarchy. Industrial workers realized their strength as a group and eventually labour unions became powerful agents of social change. The old vertical society was crumbling.

Thus, after 1800 and more particularly after 1850, new technical knowledge, new attitudes, new social institutions and processes joined together to produce an unprecedented rate of quantitative growth. What happened during the nineteenth century was relatively simple but highly revolutionary: man learned, especially in the Western world, that he could satisfy almost unlimited aspirations through his inventive genius. In the process, the foundations of the old steady state were destroyed.

The basic features of the new era are now well known. Population explosion has been the most spectacular phenomenon. It was only after several thousands of years that world population grew to 1 billion in 1850. However, from then on, 75 years were required to reach 2 billion, 37 years to get to 3 billion, and 13 years to arrive at 4 billion. World population was estimated at 3.6 billion in 1970 and, if current trends continue to prevail, it may reach nearly 7 billion in the year 2000.

Until the First World War, the population explosion was limited mainly to what we describe today as the developed countries. It was largely the product of the decline in the death rate. These nations might have been caught in the reproduction spiral, but wars and massive emigration enabled them to devote an increasing portion of their economic growth and their gains in productivity to the improvement of the standard of living which eventually brought down the birth rate. For these rather accidental reasons, exponential growth in Europe ceased to be mainly demographic after 1920. The path to rapid and intensive industrialization was opened to the developed countries.

In the underdeveloped world, the exponential era did not really begin until the 1920s. Imperialism and the growing needs of Western nations for certain agricultural products, industrial raw materials, and petroleum provided a basis for economic growth. This expansion, the progress of tropical medicine, and improved public health produced a rapid increase in life expectancy and a substantial decline in the death rate. But the outlets – particularly massive emigration – which eventually enabled Western countries to reduce their birth rate were not and probably will not be available to the so-called Third World. For this reason and others, the expectation expressed by many economists in the early 1960s that these countries would gradually follow the Western growth model seems today to be unrealistic, except for those nations in a position to use 'materials blackmail.' Most of the Third World may not reach the level of education and the standard of living required to produce naturally a substantial decline in the birth rate. Thus, their exponential growth is likely to be limited to demographic growth for the foreseeable future, unless an effective population policy is soon enforced.

The existence of the exponential era with its two quite different spirals – population and productivity – cannot be denied. Its fundamental causes are now well known: the development of technologies leading to a tremendous increase in production and a substantial decline in the death rate, the mentality of 'the commons' or man's rising expectations, and new social processes and institutions which have enabled the first two forces to assert themselves.

PHYSICAL AND TECHNOLOGICAL LIMITS TO GROWTH

Many experts have warned us for a long time that there were physical limits to growth in the world. In 1954, in his book *The Challenge of Man's Future*, Harrison Brown gave us a global view of these limits. It is only recently, however, that we have become collectively more conscious of this basic fact after a flood of reports and studies and, more importantly, the oil crisis. I do not intend here to review these physical constraints because they have been widely discussed and undoubtedly exaggerated by some during the so-called Doom Debate. I would like to suggest, however, that Canadians should not succumb to blind hopes by assuming that they have boundless resources; we should also begin to think in terms of physical limits to growth. It is true that Canada has about one-third of the world's supply of fresh water. Although portions of this supply are polluted and others not easily accessible, in the long run this may well be our most precious resource and, also, a cause of increasing contention with the United States.

There is growing evidence however, that in other ways our country is not endowed with boundless resources. Only about 7 per cent of Canada's 3.8 million square miles is suitable for agriculture and most of this area is already in use. Growing cities and suburbs, airfields, networks of highways, and recreational facilities are already depriving us rapidly of irreplaceable topsoil. The Ontario Federation of Agriculture has estimated that in that province, on the average, 26 acres of good arable land are withdrawn from agriculture every hour. If it is also true that the climate is cooling, this could be another important limiting factor for Canadian agriculture. Dr B. B. Migicovsky, director-general of the federal Department of Agriculture research branch, stated recently that prairie soil has only about two-thirds the nitrogen it had twenty years ago.

Most of our important hydraulic sites are now exploited. The others, as the James Bay project shows, will be much more expensive to develop. During the 1960s Canadians were pleading with the Americans to accept substantially higher oil imports; yet a report of the National Energy Board published in October 1974, stated that 'in the early 1980s there will no longer be sufficient availability of indigenous oil to meet Canadian feedstock requirements.'[13] In February 1975 the federal Minister of Energy warned that Canada will become a net importer of oil at the end of 1975 at the annual rate of about 200,000 barrels per day.

The Mining Committee report to the 1973 National Outlook Conference emphasized that the era of 'easy ore' was over for Canadian mining. It warned that most of the deposits which are easy to discover have been found and that the new ore would have to come from expensive frontier areas and greater depths. A recent estimate based on current exponential rates of production and Canadian known reserves, gives the expected time to depletion of such materials as: copper 18 years, iron ore 94, lead 31, nickel 23, zinc 14, asbestos 36, and potash 38 years.[14]

Most Canadians assume that our wood supply is nearly inexhaustible. However, a former spokesman for the pulp and paper industry wrote recently: 'I once estimated the wood requirements to meet the probable demand in 1990 for Canadian pulp and paper and found that in the early 1980s our supposedly inexhaustible supply of trees would be taxed to capacity ... To have enough trees to meet the demands of 1990 we ought to start planting trees this afternoon.'

These illustrations should not be interpreted as 'foreseeing doom,' but as a warning that Canadian resources are not boundless and that the present situation clearly demands foresight.

While most experts agree that there are physical limits to growth, some believe that they can be overcome almost indefinitely by technology. For instance, Alvin Weinberg, director of the Oak Ridge National Laboratory, states: 'I think we have problems, but I also think that technology has to be given a chance and the incentive and the prodding to deal with these problems.'[15] Technology has been a major factor leading to an 'open-ended' world and it could provide many other spectacular opportunities in the future. It may be argued that after 1990 the combination of fast-breeders with high-temperature gas-cooled reactors and hydrogen technology could satisfy all our energy needs. Nuclear fusion, solar energy, and other new sources also have a high technological potential. However, assuming the continuation of historical patterns of growth and ideal technological conditions of efficiency, Mesarovic and Pestel have estimated that, in one hundred years, three thousand 'nuclear parks' each consisting of eight fast-breeder reactors would be needed to satisfy world energy requirements. This would mean that we would have to build, in each and every year between now and then, four reactors per week and eventually two reactors per day simply to replace those that have worn out.[16] Such a program would create insuperable technical and financing difficulties and unbearable hazards.

The promises of new food technologies seem unlimited. Theodore Gordon mentions some of them[17]: the manufacture of fabricated foods, including meat analogues and meat extenders, new strains of bacteria for fixing nitrogen in the soil, animal hotels for efficient raising of cows and pigs, fish farming, twinning drugs to produce more than one calf per cow a year.

The 'technological fix' could go a long way to meet growing scarcities of industrial raw materials. New techniques may be developed to use the nodules forming in oceans and to use low-grade ores. Undoubtedly synthetic and substitute materials will be available in critical applications. Recycling and the production of essentially non-obsolescent goods offer almost unlimited possibilities. Though technology can work wonders, it is equally true that its indiscriminate extensive and intensive use can have most undesirable side effects and even produce catastrophes which may not be anticipated at first. The Senate Special Committee on Science Policy, in Volume 2 of its Report, has listed enough of them to show that mankind would be most unwise to rely on the technological fix to pursue exponential growth.[18]

There are limits not only to the use but also to the development of technology.

John Platt in *The Step to Man* is forecasting plateaux in the technologies of transportation, communications, weapons, and computers. The increase in life expectancy resulting from the application of new medical knowledge may also be much less substantial in the future than it has been in recent decades.[19] The development of new technologies has also financial and time limits. The cost of research and development is rising rapidly as a result of inflation and the 'sophistication factor.' On the other hand, governments, which have become the main source of funding in most countries, feel that they have other more immediate priorities. Moreover, national science policies have generally proved to be rather ineffective; they have failed to develop a coherent technological strategy oriented toward the recycle society, the exploitation and conservation of resources, and the preservation of the environment.[20]

It takes time to develop new technology, to transform it into successful innovations, and to diffuse new or improved products or processes. Sir Allan H. Cottrell claims that a lead time of about three years is required to develop a small scientific instrument and more than seven years for a subsonic jet aircraft.[21] Nuclear fission reactors became feasible during the Second World War, the first commercial reactor began to operate in 1956, but nuclear plants still experience technical difficulties today.

Thus technology, if given a chance, can certainly ease the transition between an open-ended world and a new steady state. But, given the physical limits that we have to face, it cannot indefinitely sustain the kind of undifferentiated exponential growth that we have experienced since 1800. Some of these constraints may not be immediately apparent when the potential of technology is related to only one problem. The Club of Rome has formed a group of technological optimists under the chairmanship of Denis Gabor to consider the contributions that researchers might make to the supply of materials, energy, and food. Its report which now has the temporary title of *New Directions for Science and Technology* shows that, in each of the three sectors considered in isolation, technology could be expected to make a substantial contribution; but in each field success depends on the potential of the other two, and these contributions represent new demands not now being taken into consideration.

ECONOMIC LIMITS TO GROWTH

The human limits to growth are probably the most determining and yet they have been seriously neglected in the Doom Debate. Even the two reports to the Club of Rome build their case on physical and technological limits; they prescribe an impressive list of human imperatives, but they hardly suggest how these objectives will be met.

Glenn T. Seaborg, in his article 'The Recycle Society of Tomorrow,' provides a typical illustration of the 'optimistic' view of mankind and its future. He summarizes his forecast when he says that 'sooner or later we will stabilize our population, we will minimize our environmental impact and efficiently manage our use of natural resources; and we will achieve a relatively peaceful world with a more equitable distribution of goods, services and opportunities throughout the world.' He describes 'where we might be in 1994 – assuming that most things turn out right, that cool heads, kind hearts, and common sense prevail and guide all our human assets.'[22]

Such forecasts may be interesting and comforting, but they ignore the most important part of the story, in spite of repeated warnings and the lessons of history. A. Gregg in 1955 wrote: 'The world has cancer and the cancer is man.'[23] William Saroyan warned: 'The human race is getting to be too much for itself and too much for the world.'[24] René Dubos observed: 'We dislike polluted and cluttered environments, but we like economic prosperity and gadgets even more.'[25] More recently, Robert L. Heilbroner repeated the same warning.[26]

History shows that most past civilizations declined after they had destroyed their natural environment. Plato observed in ancient Greece that 'the rich and soft soil has run off and only the emaciated skeleton of the country remains.'[27] However, other powerful forces can also be at work. Henry Pelham thus describes the decline of the Roman Republic: 'the fabric of tradition embodied in the *mos maiorum* fell to pieces; a revolt set in against Roman discipline and Roman traditions of self-effacement, and the craving for individual distinction asserted itself with irresistible vehemence ... Among the lower classes, contact with foreign slaves and freedmen, with foreign worships and foreign vices, produced a love of novelty which no legislation could check. Even amongst women there were symptoms of revolt against the old order, which showed itself in a growing freedom of manners and impatience of control, the marriage tie was relaxed, and the respect for mother and wife, which had been so powerful a factor in the maintenance of the Roman standard of morals, was grievously diminished. Thus Rome was at length brought face to face with a moral and economic crisis which a modern historian has described in the words: "Italy was living through the fever of moral disintegration and incoherence which assails all civilized societies that are rich in the manifold resources of culture and enjoyment, but tolerate few or no restraints on the feverish struggle of contending appetites" ... Political corruption was reduced to a science for the benefit of individuals who were often faced with the alternatives of ruin or revolution; there was no longer any body of sound public opinion to which, in the last resort, appeal could be made; and long before the final catastrophe took place, Roman society itself had become, in structure and temper, thoroughly unrepublican.'[28] Cato the Censor and others foresaw this disintegration. A series of measures were passed to check the growth of luxury and licence, and to exclude the foreign teachers of the new learning. But it was all in vain: Nero fiddled while Rome burned.

Human limits to growth are multiple. They are economic and social, individual and institutional, national and international.

The conventional wisdom in economics is optimistic. It says that supply will meet demand through substitution, new technology and price adjustments, provided the market mechanism is allowed to work. This is true to a large extent. However, as lower-grade resources must be exploited or as production becomes more round-about, more capital is required and costs are usually rising. As supply becomes more scarce and monopolistic, prices tend to increase rapidly. The impact of these factors and others is more substantial as physical and technological limits to growth are felt. At this juncture, the economist's model of free and perfect competition becomes even more unrealistic.

Let us take as an illustration the growing food requirements of developing countries and their financial ability to meet them. David Pimental and his co-authors assert: 'In the United States we are currently using an equivalent of 80 gallons of gasoline to produce an acre of corn. With fuel shortages and high prices to come, we wonder if many developing nations will be able to afford the technology of U.S. agriculture.'[29] There are economic limits to the growth of food production and distribution. M. Guernier in his report, 'Perspectives alimentaires de l'an 2000,' claims that the world-wide availability of food per capita has not increased since 1936 and actually decreased during the last decade.[30] In the future, under normal economic circumstances, food will become relatively scarce and expensive in the world. This will mean widespread starvation, malnutrition, and disease in many developing countries and, according to Mesarovic and Pestel, 'the death of hundreds of millions,' 'socio-political breakdowns,' and an 'unprecedented tragedy for the entire world.' Even under ideal conditions, which include effective population policies, rapid technological developments and transfers, the creation of a huge international capital pool and a world granary, the economic limits to the growth of food production and distribution will create a crucial issue for the Third World and between temperate and tropical regions.

New sources of supply of industrial raw materials and fuels will be available, but whether they come from substitutes, the exploitation of nodules or low-grade ores, the use of tar sands, nuclear or solar energy, they are likely to be more costly and to require huge amounts of capital. The recycle society is not going to be cheap and seems to raise obstacles of its own. If the world must eventually build seven nuclear power stations per week to meet additional demand or for replacement, the amounts of capital required by this program alone will be staggering.

Meanwhile, as with food, the number of countries exporting raw materials and fuels will decline and the needs of importing nations will grow. In this instance, however, the developed world will be the main consumer, although the underdeveloped regions where resources are scarce could be caught in a worse squeeze.

As supplies of industrial raw materials, natural gas, and oil become more localized in a small number of developing countries, the temptation to use monopolistic practices and 'materials blackmail' will increase. The annual excess of revenues of the OPEC countries is now estimated at $60 billion. At this rate, which corresponds to a very conservative estimate, they will accumulate an amount of $500 billion in less than ten years, which is of the same order of magnitude as the existing world monetary reserves.[31] The same strategy has been applied to phosphate and bauxite, and it may be extended to other scarce products as a response to high oil and food costs.

This sudden and revolutionary development may have a highly disrupting impact in the world. Some of the petrodollars are used by OPEC countries to increase imports aimed at promoting their own growth, to take over multinational corporations operating within their boundaries, and to provide financial aid to poor nations. They are also utilized to build their military capacity which is potentially dangerous. The recycling of petrodollars and huge chronic balance-of-payment deficits will undoubtedly represent a time-bomb which could explode at any time during the coming years and destroy world economic stability. Will the OPEC countries be willing to make huge direct investments in the developed world and will the latter accept this foreign ownership and control over its strategic industrial sectors? How will the banking system in the West be able to handle the increasing flow of short term money and live under the constant threat of sudden huge withdrawals and growing unpaid loans? What will happen if countries like Italy, Great Britain, and others facing chronic and mounting deficits are forced to declare a moratorium on the repayment of their foreign debts?

The technological fix which is promised to meet food requirements, growing scarcities of raw materials, energy and water and to maintain pollution at tolerable levels will certainly be expensive. On the whole, as we approach the economic limits to growth, we face a capital-hungry world where monopolistic groups will multiply at the national and international levels in an attempt to get for themselves as big a piece of the pie as possible. The inevitable result of these basic trends, assisted by the action of central banks, will be continuing chronic inflation.

Man has forgotten that everything is not possible immediately and at the same time. Chronic inflation is the result of collective irresponsibility and of addiction to undifferentiated growth. Together with materials blackmail and the indexing of commodity prices and incomes, it will create a new system of redistribution of wealth within and amongst nations inevitably leading to growing internal and international tensions.

SOCIO-POLITICAL AND INSTITUTIONAL LIMITS

In addition to the constraints already mentioned, we are already exposed to socio-political and institutional limits. Rising expectations and the mentality of 'the commons' are still powerful driving forces throughout the world, but the rationality on which they rest may bring much slower growth, if not ruin. Most of the developing nations, whether they live under a democratic system or a dictatorship, are becoming random societies as they continue to suffer from their population explosion.

Even the most optimistic experts who claim that there is still an immense physical and technological potential for the expansion of food production in the Third World agree that the economic, institutional, and socio-political limits are also very great. They place their hopes on the decline of the birth rate and on the essential role that developed countries could play as suppliers of food and promoters of agricultural modernization. However, they have not yet proposed a practical scheme of population control. They admit that the commitment of developed countries has been diminishing for a decade. They cannot see how these countries will agree to reduce their consumption of meat, milk, and other animal products, which require from four to seven calories of plant material for each calorie contained in them.

In addition to its own economic limits, the developed world is facing growing socio-political and institutional constraints. With greater affluence, better education, and improving communications, a growing number of individuals are becoming more conscious of their own priorities and looking for ways to realize their rising expectations.

In the private sector, an increasing number of groups, including businesses, labour and farm movements, citizens' committees, religious and ethnic groups, consumer and environmentalist associations – to name a few – seek to assert their own economic, social, and cultural aspirations. This system of countervailing forces leads to conflicts and makes national consensus much harder to achieve. As was said of ancient Rome, our civilized societies 'tolerate few or no restraints on the feverish struggle of contending appetites ... There [is] no longer any body of sound public opinion to which, in the last resort, appeal [can] be made.'

It is often asserted that we have paid lip service to participatory democracy and that it remains an empty word. This is not true if the concept is not restricted to participation in politics and is defined to cover involvement in the whole collective decision-making process. In this larger sense, participatory democracy has been rising rapidly, especially since the last World War, but it has destroyed the old consensus, and led to growing confrontation as a result of the 'feverish struggle of contending appetites.' Dissatisfaction with disrupting effects is becoming widespread. Harland Cleveland has described this recent evolution: 'Nobody could be fully in charge of anything, and the horizontal society was born.'[32]

Greater involvement in the collective decision-making process is not the only factor which has made it more complicated. As we reach the critical stage of exponential growth and as more people want to satisfy their own aspirations, they become more interdependent. The room to manoeuvre is more restricted and the sources of conflict multiply. Moreover, as Sir Geoffrey Vickers argues, the scope and range of decision-making are widening: 'There would today be no sense in arguing that there ought to be more or less rain; but there is plenty of sense in arguing that there ought to be more houses. And so soon as we come to control rainfall we shall certainly begin to argue about how much ought to fall on whom. The greater the span of human power, the greater the field of human responsibility is deemed to be, and the wider, in consequence, becomes the area in which ethical arguments can be used. So our expectations of what ought to be have grown with our concepts of what might be made to be; and the field for ethical argument has grown with them. The field of human conflict has correspondingly widened.'[33]

As these trends develop, various segments of society can find another to blame for their own problems and failures. Their frustrations lead them to appeal to the state to resolve private conflicts – which they resent as government interference if the decision is not in their favour. How can we expect the state to resolve the basic conflicts that paralyse the private decision-making process and satisfy everybody when society will 'tolerate few or no restraints on the feverish struggle of contending appetites.'? When Louis St Laurent was prime minister he once said to me: 'It is more and more impossible to keep *all* the people equally satisfied so we have to try to keep them equally *dis*satisfied.' But that attitude seriously weakens the public decision-making process. With no 'body of sound public opinion to which, in the last resort, appeal could be made,' the state cannot provide leadership and is forced instead to be a fire brigade, solving crises as they arise without the benefit of planning.

Ultimately, governments become the scapegoats of this obsessive transferring of faults. In addition, governments have developed weaknesses of their own. Growing bureaucracies fighting against each other to preserve or extend their respective territories and a time-consuming legislative process too often dominated by the negative forces of the adversary system can hardly produce imaginative, sound, and quick decisions. Federalism, in spite of its advantages, increases these deficiencies. In this age of interdependence, national governments face more problems, such as inflation, military and economic threats, pollution, which are beyond their power to solve alone. They become increasingly unstable. International institutions, including the United Nations, are caught in the conflicts of ideologies and nationalisms; they are dominated by 'the tyranny of the majority.'

Thus, in our Western societies it is the whole collective decision-making process, in the private as much as in the public sector, that suffers from growing paralysis. Government leadership is almost impossible in a democratic society without the support of a 'body of sound public opinion.' This paralysis results from socio-political limits generated by the rise of the horizontal society and the pains of uncontrolled growth.

More fundamentally, perhaps, we face institutional constraints. New institutions and social processes had reinforced technological change in the nineteenth century to launch the exponential era. They gradually helped create an open-ended system. However, these institutions have not been able to develop a capacity to handle the uncertainty and the instability they had generated. Having destroyed the old steady state through accelerated change, they have built a logic of resistance, a defence mechanism against change which Donald Schon calls 'dynamic conservatism.'[34] The widespread use of dynamic conservatism or of 'the mode of least change' means that the private and public institutions which launched the exponential era are no longer adequate to face the problems of that period and to bring mankind into another steady state. The organizational culture of least change paralyses the collective decision-making process. It tends to make established institutions increasingly irrelevant, to destroy their ideological base, and to endanger their very survival.

Ultimately, our growing socio-political constraints and the failure of our organizational culture can only be explained by the absence of a shared system of adequate values. As George Steiner noted in *Nostalgia for the Absolute*, Christian belief, practice, and thought, which pervaded and shaped Western society from the decline of the Roman world up until the last century, are for all practical effects dead. 'God is dead,' remarked Nietzsche. The heirs of the Enlightenment clung to the belief in reason, in Bentham's felicific calculus, and in the technological fix which leads eventually to the ruin of the commons and to 'an immense emptiness.' Modern herdsmen became rational individually but not collectively.

Thus, as we reassess the limits to growth, we find that the physical and technological constraints are real but not as determining as it was first thought. Economic boundaries may well be more important. However, Alexander King in his article 'The Club of Rome – Setting the Record Straight' is probably right when he writes: 'In the final analysis, the limits to growth are not material but political, social, managerial, and within the nature of man.'[35]

COPING WITH THE UNSTEADY STATE

There are still people who believe that undifferentiated exponential growth can go on more or less forever, that our planet has almost unlimited resources, that the technological fix can accomplish miracles, or that man's capacity to adjust to the exponential trajectory is boundless. These blind hopes, which are not even based on the history of past civilizations, can only lead to a 'storm of crisis problems' more difficult to solve as they are allowed to develop.

There are other people who agree that exponential quantitative growth will come to an end sooner or later but that mankind can do or will be willing to do very little to stop it in an orderly way by calculation and planning. They wonder with Norbert Wiener 'whether we may not be biologically on the way out.'[36] They have become fatalistic and cynical because they believe that man and society are incapable of meeting the demands they have created. They want to opt out and they refuse to play institutional roles which might help prevent a collective collapse.

There are others, like Lord Keynes in his *Essays on Persuasion*, who believe that exponential quantitative growth will stop before we are forced by physical, technological, or human constraints to close our open-ended world. They claim that mankind itself may bring back the steady state gradually and peacefully as the result of a natural biological and psychological rejection of growth. This scenario has been presented by John Kettle in his article, 'The Decline and Fall of Economic Growth.'[37]

There is no doubt that a social ethos against exponential quantitative growth is developing in one way or another. The work ethic is not as strong as it used to be in our affluent societies. More people want more leisure and they are learning to use it in a creative way. The ecological movement is still young, but it has already succeeded in imposing restraints on the indiscriminate application of new technology, more particularly in the United States on the construction of nuclear plants. It has also been responsible for better conservation measures and more effective pollution control.

Oriental philosophies and religions are making an increasing impact on human development in the West, emphasizing the simplicity of life, the rediscovery of awareness, contemplation, and psychological peak-experiences. It may well be that the suppliers of Western technology will increasingly become the recipients of Oriental mysticism.

However, the new social ethos and the movements just mentioned are too marginal and come too late to be able by themselves to prevent the storms ahead. They may teach us, as Christianity did in Ancient Rome, how to survive in a new equilibrium once the worst is over. They will help us to go through the watershed and to cope with the unsteady state, the uncertainties, and the turmoil it involves. But while they may prove to be useful buffers, they will not be able, if left to themselves, to guide us through these troubled waters.

During this difficult voyage, we need more people ready to do their duty toward mankind and to provide the lights which will show beyond these waters what the Sea of Tranquillity might look like. Lights are brought to the world today by an increasing number of people who are concerned and who care, who refuse blind hopes without becoming fatalistic or cynical. As a result of their message, as Margaret Mead puts it, 'this is the first time in history that man has been able to label what was happening to him while it was happening.'[38] The lights show us that we have reached a watershed, that we have to build a new steady state, and how this challenging venture can succeed.

More people are putting forward their own blueprints and models for the construction of this new balanced world. What is encouraging is the high degree of unanimity being achieved on prescriptions although various experts may emphasize different aspects. Fundamentally their approaches are complementary. They constitute the ingredients of a new manifesto which is not factional, not left or right, but human and forward. As such, it can have a universal appeal which is an essential requirement for global problems and solutions.

Much more work is required to complete the manifesto. 'Inventing the Future,' as Denis Gabor says, is not an easy challenge. The message is new and yet, as it is, it may not be as unrealistic and utopian as it sounds to the cynics or as unnecessary as it appears to those who deny the existence of the issues that we have to face. At least, it is a ray of hope for a world which greatly needs it. But we do not need only this message to reveal the location and the content of our hopeful destiny. We must have a new compass to reach it and to guide us through the troubled waters ahead. John Platt writes: 'We must continually look ahead to see which direction we are going in and how it needs to be changed, and what we must do to change it.'[39]

This new compass can only be provided by better and more systematic futures studies conducted on a multidisciplinary basis. All countries need a national coordinated network of such studies. In Canada, we must soon establish such a network with a central core which could be called the Canadian Centre for Futures Studies.

But the compass, essential as it is, is not very useful if it is not used. We also need a more responsive helm. In other words, futures studies must have a real impact on the making of both private and public decisions so as to render them less self-centred and short-sighted. Experience shows that such an outcome cannot be spontaneous. All countries need coupling mechanisms and institutions mediating between futures research and decision-making. In Canada, we must establish a relaying and rallying network on the future composed of as many private and public organizations as possible with a central station which could be called Futures Canada. This other new anticipatory institution would, amongst its various functions, gather, store, and diffuse significant results of futures studies carried out in Canada and abroad to its network of organizations; it would also organize periodic meetings of public and private institutions committed to future-oriented thinking as a first step toward a continuing plebiscite on the future, a more elaborate form of 'anticipatory democracy,' and a future-oriented consensus.

The need for such an anticipatory institution has become urgent. For the function of management is essentially to probe the future. The dictum *'gouverner c'est prévoir'* applies not only to governments but also to the private sector. Thus it is necessary to provide better, more usable information on alternative futures in order to improve organizational decision-making.

It is even more important to organize and maintain what Alvin Toffler calls 'a continuing plebiscite on the future'[40] in an attempt to develop a 'body of sound public opinion,' to arrive at a future-oriented consensus, and to overcome the paralysis of the collective decision-making process. If our horizontal society is to work and cope with the mounting problems of the unsteady state, it must be complemented by anticipatory democracy.

Claude Gruson, a former influential French public servant, notes that the mounting problems caused by exponential growth and its eventual collapse will require collective long-term decisions difficult to imagine, to accept, and to launch, and attaches a great importance to the continuing plebiscite: 'the organization of the debate holds a crucial place. It is this debate which must identify conflicts, prepare the bases of agreements or delimit disagreements, and which must in any case allow each interested party to understand the nature of the problems raised, to design the solutions which appear the best to him, to measure his agreement and disagreement with the solution being implemented, and to evaluate the political importance of this agreement or disagreement.'[41]

Futures Canada will not accomplish miracles. However, if it is organized efficiently, if it uses the best techniques of information technology, and if its membership represents a good sample of the various segments of Canadian society, it can help develop long-term assessments and launch the continuing plebiscite which could lead to 'mutual persuasion.' It must be seen as a seed operation which could start the amplification process and what John Platt calls 'a social chain-reaction with positive feedback.' Many countries, including Canada, have reached the stage where such an operation could have a large multiplier effect.

The challenge of the next twenty-five years will be decisive. As the Prime Minister, Pierre E. Trudeau, said in his speech at Duke University in May 1974:

'The challenge is immense, and I am glad that it is, for only the greatest of challenges are able to capture the imagination of men and women everywhere. The challenge is at once both basic and sophisticated and I am glad that it is, for only a challenge of many parts is able to stimulate simultaneously the response of theologians, philosophers, scientists, and politicians. The challenge is not a gloomy one of avoiding doomsday; it is a joyous one of introducing into the world a dynamic equilibrium between man and nature, between man and man.'

NOTES

1 *The Limits to Growth* (Washington, DC, 1972)
2 A great number of critical reviews have been published. One of the most serious which contains numerous references has been prepared by the Science Policy Research Unit of Sussex University: *Thinking about the Future: A Critique of the Limits to Growth* (Toronto, 1973).
3 *The Biology of Population Growth* (New York, 1925)
4 'Nuclear energy and the fossil fuels,' in American Petroleum Institute, *Drilling and Production Practice* (1956), pp. 7-25
5 *Essays in Persuasion* (New York, 1932), p. 372
6 (Cambridge, 1960)
7 'Survey of world energy resources,' *Canadian Mining and Metallurgical (CIM) Bulletin,* July 1973, p. 53
8 *The Coming of the Golden Age* (1969)
9 Mihajlo Mesarovic and Eduard Pestel, *Mankind at the Turning Point* (Toronto, 1974)
10 *Les 40,000 heures* (Paris, 1965)
11 These figures and many others are presented by John McHale in 'World Facts and Trends,' *Futures,* vol. 3, no. 3 (Sept. 1971), pp. 216-301.
12 *Science* (Dec. 1968), p. 1244
13 *In the Matter of the Exportation of Oil* (Ottawa), p. 6-2
14 These estimates, based on available official data, have been prepared by Mr Philip Pocock, research director, Senate Special Committee on Science Policy.
15 Remark made during a dialogue with Prof. Barry Commoner in, 'Must the world take a power cut?' from 'The Great Doom Debate' originally published in the *Observer,* London, March 1972
16 Mesarovic and Pestel, *Mankind at the Turning Point,* p. 132
17 'Some crises that will determine the world of 1994,' *The Futurist,* vol. VIII, no. 3, June 1974, p. 117

18 Senate Special Committee on Science Policy, *Targets and Strategies for the Seventies*, vol. 2, Ottawa, 1972, chap. II
19 (New York, 1966), pp. 187-95
20 This statement is based on the evidence presented by the Senate Special Committee on Science Policy, more particularly in volumes 1 and 3 of its Report.
21 'Technological Thresholds,' *The Process of Technological Innovation*, National Academy of Sciences, Washington, DC, 1969
22 *The Futurist*, vol. VIII, no. 3 (June 1974), p. 108
23 'A medical aspect of the population problem,' *Science*, 121, p. 681
24 Quoted by Mesarovic and Pestel, *Mankind at the Turning Point*, p. 130
25 *Reason Awake* (New York, 1970), p. 127
26 *An Inquiry into the Human Prospect* (New York, 1974)
27 Quoted by Rolf Edberg, *On the Shred of a Cloud* (University of Alabama Press, 1969), p. 133; translated into English from *Spillran av ett Moln* (Stockholm, 1966)
28 *Encyclopedia Britannica*, vol. 19, p. 490
29 'Food production and the energy crisis,' in *Energy: Today's Choices, Tomorrow's Opportunities*, edited by Anton B. Schmalz (World Future Society, Washington, 1974)
30 Personal report to the Club of Rome, 1974
31 These figures are presented by Mesarovic and Pestel, *Mankind at the Turning Point*, pp. 22 and 26.
32 'How do you get everybody in on the act and still get some action?,' *Educational Record*, vol. 55, no. 3, 1974 (American Council on Education, Washington, DC), p. 177
33 *Making Institutions Work* (London, 1973), pp. 12 and 13
34 *Beyond the Stable State* (London, 1971), chap. 2
35 *The Center Magazine*, vol. 7 (Sept.-Oct. 1974), p. 22
36 Quoted by Dubos, *Reason Awake*, p. 125
37 *New Scientist*, 19 Dec. 1974, pp. 876-7
38 'Ways to deal with the current social transformation,' *The Futurist*, vol. VIII, no. 3 (June 1974), p. 122
39 'World transformation: changes in belief systems,' *ibid.*, p. 125
40 *Future Shock* (New York, 1970)
41 'Réplique aux objecteurs de croissance,' *Expansion*, juillet-août 1972

'Terra incognita' and the economist's compass

A. W. JOHNSON

New perspectives for economic policy

There is no novelty to the notion that values other than economic ones ought to occupy a central place in the social, economic, and political systems of the world. Equity and justice, individual development and self-fulfilment, peace and beauty, are not after all new ideas. But that economic growth and increases in material well-being should actually be abated, if necessary, in order to give a more fitting place to these other values is indeed a novel assertion in the perspective of these times.

Nor indeed can it truthfully be said any longer that there is much novelty to the proposition that the Western world can no longer preoccupy itself primarily with economic growth, even if it wanted to. The consequences of growth, most spectacularly the damage to the environment and the rising costs of scarce resources in developed countries, together with the pressure for a larger share of growth and the fruits of growth on the part of countries with burgeoning populations but small incomes, are combining to challenge the paramountcy which has been attached to industrial growth by and for the developed countries. Thus the question of what kind of society might emerge, or better still ought to emerge, where the objective of industrial growth comes to occupy a less dominant position than it has in relation to other values or other problems, has come to occupy the minds of those who are trying to look beyond the immediate issues of the day.

I am afraid that economics has not always contributed as much as it might to the problem of perceiving and balancing the many values which motivate a society. Nor has it always recognized or sought to comprehend within its systems the major forces or problems other than the economic which are moving societies.

For an economist to try to say something, therefore, about the question of 'New Perspectives for Economic Policy' is a forbidding assignment. It is all the more so for a person who can more accurately be described as a former practitioner in the field of economic policy and who, I should remind you, remains encumbered with all the constraints attendant upon being a public servant.

To attempt this assignment, however, is the risk and the responsibility I have assumed. I shall avoid, as a public servant, speaking out on contemporary issues in such a way as to appear to be criticizing, or for that matter prescribing, public policies, and certainly I shall avoid any inference about the rights and wrongs of the perspectives or the programs of present or former politicians. But I shall not avoid, and I do not believe ministers of the Crown any longer expect public servants to avoid, saying something about the dilemmas of public policy, no matter what the origin or the occasion of such dilemmas.

ECONOMIC AND OTHER VALUES, OTHER OBJECTIVES, OTHER IMPERATIVES

I have lamented the failure of contemporary economists to take into adequate account other values, other objectives, even other imperatives than the economic ones. This has not always been the case: the classical economists did seek to bring within the purview of their systems what they perceived as being the major social and political, as well as economic, forces of their times. I refer, of course, to Adam Smith, Ricardo and Malthus, John Stuart Mill, Marx, and more latterly Schumpeter. Even Alfred Marshall, the father of micro-economic theory, proclaimed: 'The economist, like everyone else, must concern himself with the ultimate aims of man.'

But somehow in the course of applying Keynes, and developing the new economics, we seem to have lost our way. Joan Robinson has written that 'economic theory ... for the second time (the first time being the pre-Keynesian period) has nothing to say on the questions that, to everyone except economists, appear to be most in need of an answer.'[1] Scott Gordon suggests that this failure finds its roots in even earlier times: 'that interest in these "grand" issues [he is speaking of the social questions raised by the stationary state] faded from economic theory along with the "neoclassical" development of an effective analytical apparatus for solving small problems.'[2] It was really only Boulding who perceived in recent times potential limits to levels of consumption and who sounded a warning about population growth, about possible limits on the production of food, and about the 'squandering of our geological capital.'[3]

Economics in Canada as elsewhere, in short, seems to have been drifting farther away from the 'grand issues.' We were preoccupied with stable economic growth:

first with stability, then with growth, and then with prescribing a growth path and how to stay on it. We were preoccupied with the trade-off between unemployment and inflation in achieving this optimum growth: of determining where the 'Phillips curve' was, considering how it could be shifted, and finally puzzling over whether it could be said to exist at all. We were consumed with our econometric models and our capacity to predict the future of the economy; with the functions in our models and their steady refinement; with the meticulous measurement of leads and lags; and with the capacity of our models to predict the impact on the economy of various kinds and degrees of stimulus and restraint.

In the field of international trade, a favourite field for Canadians, and understandably so, we pursued our continuing preoccupation of creating in the real world the free markets we had learned about and taught in economic theory. We pressed for a floating exchange rate rather than a fixed one: it would facilitate trade and relax the external constraints on domestic macro-economic policies. We called for a new unit of international exchange and for greater international liquidity: they would facilitate the freedom of trade which a market economy called for. And we supported tariff reductions and the elimination of quotas and embargos for the same good reason.

In the field of public finance, aside from macro-economic theory and policy, we concentrated our efforts on bringing within our theoretical framework or on extending it to embrace issues and decisions which remained stubbornly outside the market system. We refined the theory of public goods. We recognized the social costs of certain of the by-products of economic growth, and sought to find ways of bringing the producers of these undesirable by-products to pay for them. We recognized too the growing impact of government decisions – so utterly outside the market system – and sought to apply our analytical skills to explaining, or better still rationalizing, public policy decisions. Hence cost-benefit analysis, planning, programming and budgeting, zero-base budgeting, and the sometimes elaborate if still limited theories of decision-making.

And all of this went on together with the exploration and elaboration of pure economic theory. Much of what was done by the economists was, of course, sound scholarship and ultimately good public policy. It remains, however – to sum up these shortcomings in a sweeping generalization – that much of what we did was to seek to force into the mould of our market theory and related models the phenomena which clearly fell outside of them. Alternatively, if that didn't work, we ignored these phenomena as falling beyond the ken of economics.

What we failed to do, in short, and what others began to do for us, was to recognize and seek to cope with the emerging global issues in their full dimension; to reckon with the increasing insistence on the part of peoples and nations that values other than purely economic ones should rank and compete with the ethos of the industrial society; and to take into account the institutional changes, domestic and international, which were creating forces of compelling importance, both public and private, but which operated outside of the market system and market logic.

Thus it has fallen largely to others – in company, it must in fairness be said, with some of the wiser as well as some of the younger economists – to identify and to seek to grapple with some of the grander issues. Sometimes these others have seemed to be cranks, as Joan Robinson has observed. But then, to use her words, the cranks flourish 'because the orthodox economists have neglected the great problems that everyone else feels to be urgent and menacing.'[4]

THE GRAND ISSUES

What then are these great problems, these grand issues? They are by now known to us all: well identified by the scholars and practitioners who have been writing about the limits to growth, about the post-industrial society, and about the drift towards, or the prescription for, a stationary state. I am speaking, of course, of people like Jay W. Forrester, D.H. Meadows and the other authors of the Club of Rome's *The Limits to Growth*, Robert L. Heilbroner, and others who have concerned themselves with the individual issues or problems which combine to form the proposition that infinite growth is not possible in a finite world.[5]

These issues are by now common knowledge: a burgeoning population, particularly in those parts of the globe least able to support more people; limits on arable land and on the capital which can be applied to increase agricultural production; the depletion of resources at rates which are high and which would have to be increased to seemingly unattainable levels if the economic growth of western nations were to be generalized around the globe; pollution and the degrading of the environment; and the failure to bring technology to bear upon the resolution of these problems in time to render them tolerable.

There are in addition to these primary or fundamental problems, the problems which flow from them: the famine and the foreboding found in large areas of the globe; the increasing tensions between the rich and the poor nations of the world; and the menace of inflation in developed and developing nations alike.

In recounting these global issues it is not my intention to recite, or in any way to appear to accept, the Club of Rome litany about cataclysmic collapse – the proposition that exponential growth in population, food consumption, industrial growth, resource use, and environmental degradation will lead to a global collapse – unless we accept *now* a zero growth goal. I agree with the critics that there are in fact 'regulators' – the price mechanism and other regulatory instruments –

which are operating or can be brought into play in such a way as to render questionable the soundness, and the direness, of the projections of the Club of Rome. And I agree with the critics who suggest that the social stresses which would be the consequence of an abrupt and almost necessarily authoritarian imposition of a no-growth policy would lead to an earlier and perhaps equally cataclysmic collapse as that which the Club of Rome has predicted after the year 2000.

But even more to the point is the fact that one does not need to accept the Club of Rome model, or their predictions, to accept the fact that they have indeed identified the major problems or issues confronting mankind. We are, in fact, already facing precisely these issues - sometimes in miniature, sometimes partially, sometimes in microcosm.

The question for economists, then, at least so it seems to me, is not whether these *are* the great issues the world does and will confront, but what economics has to say about them. At the very least, what can the profession say about the consequences which might be expected to flow from these problems, either as a result of the problems themselves, or as a consequence of different policy prescriptions designed to cope with them? More, what light can be thrown upon the issues themselves, or upon their potential resolution, by economic theory and economic policy? Conversely, what will be the impact upon economics of these compelling forces, as economists come more and more to attempt to contribute to their analysis and resolution?

These are the questions to be asked, it seems to me, about each of the major problems which has been identified for us.

Population growth
Let me begin with population growth, undoubtedly the most fundamental issue of them all. There are about four billion people in the world today. One third of them are estimated to be undernourished - which is to say 50 to 60 per cent of the peoples of less developed nations. By the year 2000 or thereabouts - twenty-five years from now - the population can be expected to rise to around six and a half billion unless there are dramatic changes in fertility rates.[6]

The capacity of the world to feed a rapidly increasing population is limited - limited by the amount of arable land, limited by the rate at which technology can be brought to bear on increasing agricultural production, and limited by the rate at which increases in capital, largely in the form of fertilizers and cultivation practices, can be brought to bear upon the production of food.

It would take extreme optimism - even irresponsible optimism - to suggest that a population growing at this order of magnitude can indeed be fed, at adequate levels, if we simply work hard at it and hope for the best. One would have to predict success in relevant technological developments, success in the opening up of new land to agricultural production, success in the application of capital to land, success in the timing of these changes in relation to the timing of population increases, and success in persuading the 'agri-powers' to transfer their food to the less fortunate peoples.

Now my question: what do the economists have to say about all of this? One thing which is sure - it became evident long ago - is that we will no longer seek to emulate Malthus by treating population as simply a dependent variable in our economic system. The manifest growth of social conscience, indeed of a world conscience, ruled that out decades ago. Nor I hope will we seek to elaborate upon newer theories which would seem to bring the fertility rate largely within our economic system, and presumably thus to mitigate the need for 'non-market intervention' - for example, the theory that a sufficiently high standard of living or an increasing participation of women in the labour force will by themselves reduce the fertility rate. There scarcely is time to wait for this, in any global perspective.

What must be done, it seems too evident to say, is that economists must recognize rather more fully, as they have done previously in other contexts, that population growth is one of the great exogenous forces with which they must cope - and cope not as part of their economic systems, but as lying alongside them, and having an enormous impact upon them.

The economist, for example, might do more to seek to determine the economic consequences of the developed countries accepting population growth as given, and increasing their food production, along with that of the less developed countries, to feed the people of those countries. In Canada, this would mean examining the shifts of capital and technological development from other purposes to the objectives of increasing food production for export abroad. The consequences would be measured, of course, in terms of a relative reduction in the production by Canadians of other goods, and, if the export of food were not fully paid for by the import of other goods Canadians wanted, by a reduction in the consumption of other products by Canadians. The economist similarly would seek to determine the effect upon agricultural prices of effecting this shift in resources and of opening up to production more marginal land. Alongside these economic consequences would have to be placed the social adjustments which would be called for, notably the readiness of Canadians to adjust to a lower rate of growth and relatively lower consumption levels, in favour of a transfer of resources to the production of food for export to the hungry of the world.

The other solution to the population problem is more the province of other social scientists: that of trying to bring population growth under control. This would be accomplished, of course, by greater emphasis upon lowering birth rates and raising the age of marriage. Here the consequences to be measured would be found more in the less developed countries than in the developed ones: the social consequences of attempting to change the values and mores of the peoples there and of changing the demographic composition and geographic distribution within the countries concerned. But there would be some adjustments in the developed countries too, if they were to shift their foreign aid more in the direction of promoting and exporting birth control devices, along with the family education which must go with them.

My point, however, is not to prescribe alternative population policies. Rather it is to argue that it is to problems like population growth that economists should increasingly apply their skills. And it is to argue that in doing so they will have to concern themselves more than they have with non-economic values, non-economic behavioural and institutional patterns, and non-economic, non-market solutions to the problems.

Non-renewable resources
The second of these great problems is the limit, as it has been described, upon the earth's non-renewable resources, including of course fossil fuels. The proposition which has been put is, again, straightforward: if the rate of industrial growth continues at past rates, and is generalized around the globe so as ultimately to provide a 'western standard of living' to all the people of the world – assuming population increases of the magnitude I have just mentioned – there simply won't be enough non-renewable resources to do the job. Not, at least, at prices which are consonant with growth at these rates.

Here, of course, the economist feels more at home. For what is economics all about if it is not about the allocation of scarce resources? Moreover, it is indeed the economist who described how growth came about – by the application of capital and labour to resources – and who developed theories about how the market mechanism allocates capital and labour and resources to the production of alternative products.

The question raised by the Club of Rome, however, is whether the market mechanism will in fact serve to regulate growth, resource use, and pollution – given the population to be 'served' by growth – along a steady path to ever new and viable equilibriums. Their answer, generally, is no: the passion for growth will lead to an 'overshoot' in the use of resources and in pollution, followed by some kind of collapse of the system.

Economists generally have rejoined that the Club of Rome spokesmen have got it all wrong: that they haven't built into their model the price 'regulators' which would bring about viable equilibriums, 'as we go' so to speak. Moreover, the economists say, the price mechanism will operate so as to increase the production of required resources – from newly discovered reserves, from lower-grade or less economic reserves, from the application of new technology to production, and from the recycling of waste. This same mechanism will operate in such a way as to bring about the substitution of lower cost resources (even new ones), the more efficient and more sparing use of scarce resources, and an increase in the durability of the goods produced from scarce resources.

All of this undoubtedly is true, given the smooth operation of the market model, and given the assumption upon which it is based. The question to be raised, I suppose, is what happens to the smooth functioning of the model when the market system does not operate as predicted – where, as Galbraith says, the economic decisions taken are essentially 'planned' corporate or governmental decisions, rather than 'market' decisions.[7] And if non-renewable resources are produced in substantial measure by multinational corporations and by governments, operating in Galbraith's planning system rather than in the pure (or purer) market system – as surely is the case – then what happens when there are major institutional or behavioural changes on the part of the corporations and the governments involved?

Unhappily we know what the answer is. There can be enormous increases in prices, by reason of the power of the participants in the market to set prices. These price increases may be a part of, or beyond, those which are brought about by discontinuities in the market, particularly those on the supply side. Petroleum prices represent the special case which make this point most vividly, but it must not be forgotten that the prices of other resources have risen too: the price index for non-ferrous metals was about 70 per cent higher at the end of 1973 than a year earlier; lumber prices at the end of 1973 were averaging 50 per cent above those at the end of 1972; and the New York price for natural rubber trebled in two years, to give but three examples.

The point of all this, of course, is that instititutional and behavioural changes, particularly in Galbraith's 'planning system,' can force on nations adjustments which are far from smooth, adjustments which are beyond those anticipated by any market model – a model which by its very nature does not incorporate institutional and behavioural changes of this order.

The utter importance of this omission is to be seen in the special case of the petroleum price increases which began in early 1974. It has been estimated that if the average price of Middle East oil remained at about $10 per barrel, the oil-importing countries of the world would pay the OPEC countries a total of $600 billion over the five years 1975 through 1979. It is further estimated that $150 to $200 billion of this amount can be covered by the export of goods and services, but that the rest – $400 to $450 billion – will have to be covered by the transfer of claims (largely, presumably, the investment by the OPEC countries of this amount in the oil-consuming countries).[8]

Now the impact of this change, in the aggregate, is serious enough: each year tens of billions of dollars of consumer payments for oil will be withdrawn from the consumption of other products in oil-consuming countries, and made available to the OPEC countries for investment, in one form or another, in one part of the world or another. But when you consider the impact upon individual countries – in particular the impact upon industrialized countries which are unable to expand their exports quickly enough to pay for their petroleum needs and don't get from the OPEC countries balancing capital inflows, and the impact upon the less developed countries who simply have no other recourse but to seek aid to pay for their oil and other resource needs – the adjustment required becomes almost mind-boggling. It no longer, in consequence, is seen as particularly radical to predict that growth rates in certain countries will almost certainly be reduced to zero, or indeed to negative rates, for at least a period of time.

What are decision-makers to do about all this? Should, for example, the countries which cannot export or borrow enough to pay for their industrial petroleum requirements be helped by the other more fortunate nations? And *within* countries which are reduced to zero or negative growth rates, should those who are hardest hit by this stagnation – obviously the poor and the weak – be assisted by their higher income compatriots? And within a country like Canada, should the concern for future generations of Canadians bring us to conserve rather than to exploit our resources, and thus to limit their export to nations in current need of them?

Adversity, in short, invokes choices between economic and other values – in particular the choice between compassion for the less fortunate nations of the world on the one hand and optimization of one's economic growth on the other. Again, these choices are made not in the market system of economic theory, but by the planning system – essentially by governments, in this case. Within this planning system, if it is institutionalized – in this case at the international level – there may be another kind of market, if you prefer to think in these terms. That is the market of values, of traditions, of power, of fear, of bargaining – whatever ethical and behavioural forces enter into decision-making within this institutional framework. If there is no such framework the decisions will be made anyway, unilaterally or bilaterally or by power blocs, and economic mechanisms will force the adjustments which are required in consequence of the decisions having thus been taken.

The point to be made, in short, is this: both population growth and the rate of use of resources – two of the great problems confronting the world – involve institutional and behavioural issues, as well as choices between non-economic and economic values. And economists will have to decide whether to content themselves with treating these as externalities, and with tracing through the economic consequences of these institutional changes and these choices between values, once identified by others, or whether they will seek to relate their discipline to – indeed adapt it to take account of – these fundamental forces.

There are, of course, economists who are attempting to do just this. There is, it must be acknowledged for example, an increasing recognition that externalities and non-market allocation are the norm and pure market allocation the exception. And there is a growing literature on the organization and behaviour of firms, bureaucracies, governments, and even the political process as a whole, designed to develop theories about non-market decisions. But it remains that the market model endures as the basic analytical apparatus of the economist, and that the economists' studies of non-market forces too often tend to resemble the market model – the bedrock of his theory – rather than the real world around him.

Would it be too cruel to recall, in this context, that almost no economists – or social scientists of any kind for that matter – foresaw the formation of OPEC and all that flowed from it? One is tempted to observe that if we as social scientists were to be surprised by too many occurrences which in retrospect seemed obvious – in the current case the use by nation states of their economic power – one would be driven to the conclusion that something was indeed missing from our analytical equipment.

Pollution
The third great issue raised by those who are writing and thinking about the post-industrial society – and indeed by a great many others – is pollution. Again the proposition which has been advanced can be simply put: high rates of industrial growth exact a heavy price in pollution – pollution of the air, of water, and of soil, and pollution of sight, sound, and smell.

Some express this price in catastrophic terms: that, for example, 'the length of life of the biosphere as an inhabitable region for organisms is to be measured in decades rather than in hundreds of millions of years.'[9] Others express it in terms of the real and measurable costs which will have to be incurred to control pollution: the cost of nuclear, then solar, power instead of that generated by fossil fuels; the cost of controlling emissions into the air and into water; the cost of new technology for increasing agricultural production at lower rates of pollution, and the rest. Still others express the price of pollution in terms of social costs – some even contemptuously, when they speak of 'the middle classes who interpreted environmentalism to mean that other people should not disturb their peace and solitude ...'[10]

Wherever one's views may fall in this spectrum, it must, it seems to me, be conceded that the more alarmist predictions are overstated given the real limits in our knowledge as to the impact upon the biosphere of different kinds of pollutants. It remains, however, that the environmentalists have caused industrialized nations to face up to the social costs which are inherent in industrial growth, and have brought them to seek a better balance as between the value of quality of life and the value of economic growth.

The data demonstrate that this balance does and will bring with it real economic costs. The U S Council on Environmental Quality has estimated (December 1974), for example, that that country's 'pollution control expenditures are heading rapidly from a 1973 level of $30 to $40 per capita to a 1976 level of $80 a person.'[11] Expenditures of this order would scarcely be undertaken if purity of the environment were merely a hobby of teary-eyed middle-class liberals.

It should be recalled, I think, that economists have, over the years, devoted a good deal of intellectual effort to coping with the question of the social costs which arise from industrial production – their so-called externalities – costs which generally are borne not by those who produce the pollution or by those who consume the products of those who pollute, but rather by the community generally. And they – the economists – have had a considerable effect upon public policy. It is instructive to consider why they have had so much to say on this issue, and with such great effect, compared with some of the other issues. My explanation, as by now I am sure you will have guessed from my earlier analysis, is that they perceived there were forces at work outside their pure market model and attempted to reckon with them. They perceived that there were values other than economic growth – call it quality of life if you will; that there were choices to be made in weighing the relative importance of the two values; that they, the economists, could contribute to the making of the decisions by determining the relative cost of each alternative, and who would benefit and who would pay under each; and, finally, that once the choice had been made, there were different public policy mechanisms for bringing it into effect.

Where some of the more theoretical economists went awry, I think, was in their effort to bring the whole thing into their market model – to make, as I have said, the whole system look as much like the neo-classical economic system as possible. I see this as a short-coming for three main reasons: it diverts the social scientist from the explicit recognition that competing values are involved in choices of this kind; it beclouds the fact that the choices to be made are not economic but normative ones – however much the costs of the options may be measured in economic terms; and it deflects attention from the fact that the choices which finally *are* made will be influenced substantially by the changing attitudes and institutions of the community.

And there is one more important point to be made about thinking in terms of 'internalizing the externalities': it obscures the fact that, because of the true nature of the decisions to be made, and the fact that they are made in Galbraith's 'planning system' as opposed to the 'market system,' those who wish to proselytize, whether they be community leaders or professional politicians, are in a position to effect changes in community attitudes and values if they want, and thus to bring about the desired changes in corporate or government behaviour.

What I am trying to say is that, when it comes to choices between values, what is needed is a larger 'social model,' so to speak, of which the economist's model would form only a part. Only in this way, it seems to me, can social scientists expect to comprehend the whole sweep of the social, political, and economic decision-making which is involved in the 'grand issues' of the times.

But I will come back to this later, when I attempt to generalize on the analysis I am trying to advance.

Growth in developed and less-developed countries
This line of reasoning might better be illustrated, I think, if I were to shift from what seems to me to be the relatively straightforward issue of pollution - not easy, but straightforward - to the more difficult one of the distribution of growth, or the fruits of growth, between the developed and the less developed countries of the world. This issue is more readily recognized, I suppose, when it is expressed in plainer if more old-fashioned terms: the distribution of income between the rich and the poor peoples of the world.

I alluded to this when discussing population growth, but now I should like to commend it to more careful consideration. For in this question, as with the question of the distribution of income within a nation, I perceive the starkest contrast as between economic and non-economic values and hence the most difficult issue confronting society. Indeed, if I were to turn into a 'doomsdayer' - which I am far from being - it would be on this question.

The root of the growing tensions between the developed and the less developed countries of the world is, of course, the enormous disparity between their incomes, and the equally troubling disparity between their respective rates of growth - a problem, one is tempted to observe, which Canadians ought readily to recognize and understand. The governments of the less developed countries not only perceive these disparities; they are determined to see them remedied. They want a share of our growth, a share of our technology, a share of our wealth, a share of our status and power. And they want it through real 'transfers of growth,' not through transfers of food and aid alone. Like everyone else, I guess, they don't want charity: they want to earn their way. But to do this they need access to the markets of the developed and developing countries, and help in establishing the industries which will produce what these markets demand.

The developed countries, in turn, not unnaturally lean towards the *status quo*, qualified by an expression, in the form of aid, of their concern for the weal of the peoples of the poorer countries. The extent of the aid has not so far been troublesome: the goal still being advocated, but not yet being realized, is to share with these countries 1 per cent of the gross national product of the developed countries. And a part of this comes back to the donors in any event, in the form of purchases under 'tied aid.'

It is one thing, however, to share one's wealth in the form of aid, but something rather more to share one's growth. Sharing one's wealth consists of transferring real resources to the poorer countries, in the form of food and raw materials, equipment, technology, and services, by giving them dollars with which to buy these goods and services from the developed countries, including Canada. But sharing one's growth calls for a greater sacrifice: it involves the opening of Canadian markets to the exports from the less developed countries, exports which may well have been produced from the very plant and technology we gave them. So their textiles, the products from their cottage industries, their other output, come to replace in our markets at least some Canadian-made products, and so reduce production and jobs.

In the longer run, of course, this reduction in gross domestic product ought to be made up: as the income of the less developed countries rises, they will be able to buy more of what we produce, and production and jobs will increase in Canada. But in the short run there are real costs involved in transferring growth to the less developed countries: a reduction of production and of jobs in Canada, as I have said, in favour of creating production and jobs in the poorer nations.

This inevitably brings in its train social adjustments for us. There would be more unemployed who would have to be supported by income security payments of some kind, or, as society increasingly views income from employment as superior to straight income transfers, they would have to be given jobs – jobs which are created for them, likely for the production of services rather than goods. There would be lower rates of growth, which would put pressure on lower-income Canadians, now less able to count upon increases in the GNP to ease their burden, which in turn would generate greater demand for increased redistribution of income.

Internationally, of course, the consequences, indeed the objective, of these transfers of growth is to build up international goodwill, and to generate a greater promise for peace and international harmony. But even here there is a price to be paid. The gradual build-up of the economic strength of the less developed countries, relative to that of the developed countries, leads to a corresponding shift in world power, with all the adjustments which inevitably ensue. It reminds one of the major increases in the late 1960s in the federal equilization payments to Canada's poorer provinces: in time the payments came to be regarded as a right, and the provinces receiving them, greatly strengthened in fiscal terms, began joining the richer provinces in challenging the policies and even the jurisdiction of the federal government.

Given the consequences of transferring economic growth to the less developed countries, how tempting for the developed countries to point out to the less developed ones that in no small measure their problems are of their own making! Put in simple arithmetic terms, per capita income can be increased either by increasing the income, or by reducing the population among which it must be divided. To do the former, through transfers from the developed countries, requires economic and social adjustments on their part, while to do the latter requires social adjustments, in the form of a more active and effective population policy, on the part of the less developed countries. How much adjustment should properly be expected from each?

All of this is so obvious, you may well say, as to raise the question as to why I am belabouring it. My answer is simple: here is writ large the choice between values – between Canada's economic growth on the one hand, and human compassion and the search for peace on the other. Here too is writ large the force of institutional and behavioural changes – the impact of communications and of international organizations upon the perception of disparities by less developed nations, and the impact of a growing world conscience upon the behaviour of more highly developed nations. Here finally is writ large the lesson for economists: the major decisions confronting the world lie outside our pure market model, and only by recognizing this, and seeking, as I have said, to comprehend our discipline within some larger model of social, political, and economic decision-making, will we make the full contribution we are capable of making to the development of public policy conclusions.

There is something to be learned from this issue, too, on the part of those who must balance economic policy with other public policies. Not only are the choices to be made in making the big decisions difficult; they may not even be perceived at all. This can occur for a number of reasons: because the 'ethical' value of the peoples of one nation having some sense of responsibility for those of another is not felt; or because the hazards of not heeding the needs of less developed nations are not recognized; or because the relative problems of the less developed countries and those of one's own nation are not comprehended. In this case it will be left to the forces of international power and conflict to bring about the adjustments which finally are made.

When the choices to be made, however, are perceived by the policy-makers, but the imperatives of those choices have not penetrated the public consciousness, then another kind of issue emerges. Does the enlightened policy-maker seek to impose upon his electors the choice he feels must be made; or does he seek to proselytize so as to bring them to recognize the imperatives he perceives; or does he simply respond to the 'political market' - as some economic theorists like to call the political process - and refrain from making the tough choices until they become evident by reason of impending disaster?

Each of these courses will bring with it, in turn, its own institutional and behavioural result and response. In the larger social, political, and economic perspective - in the larger decision-making model if you will - neither values nor institutional and behavioural forces can be taken as given, as economic theorists and practitioners have tended too often to do. Policy makers, economic policy practitioners, and social scientists alike, must recognize that the methods by which choices are made as between values and in response to institutional forces will themselves have an impact, an impact not only upon the choice which is made, but also upon the values and the institutional forces themselves.

Inflation and the distribution of income in developed countries

The fifth and last grand issue to which I should like to address myself is inflation and the distribution of income in developed and developing countries. For each of us there is to be found in this issue, in a more immediate and a more personal way than in the others, the real impact upon economic theory and policy of institutional and behavioural changes, and of the choices which must be made between economic and other values. Equally it reflects most clearly for Canadians the failure of economic theory, and the policy it prescribes, to take these forces into account. Finally, there is to be found in inflation and the distribution of income the reflection, even the culmination, of the domestic consequences of the global issues I have been discussing.

The issue of inflation is this: price rises now are proceeding at a pace which is higher than any which has ever been acceptable to Canadians. They are leading to disequilibria which are hostile to a stable economy and society, and to shifts in the distribution of income which can only serve further to reinforce the disequilibria. Macro-economic theory and policy - the so-called new economics - has not been able to provide an adequate prescription for curing the problem. Moreover, this inflation is occurring in company with very high rates of unemployment - a combination which almost any past positioning of the Phillips curve would not have contemplated. So macro-economic theorists are doubly confounded.

In extenuation of the apparent failure of economics to find a solution to this problem, it must be said that much of the inflation is occurring for external reasons - most of them having to do with the forces we have just been considering. The price of resources has been rising at unprecedented rates, in part because of growing demand, but in larger part because of the position of power enjoyed and now exercised by the oil producers. The prices of agricultural commodities have been rising, in part because of the demand-supply situation but in part also because the producers have been finding more effective ways of transferring price-fixing from their market systems to Galbraith's planning system. And there are the very substantial increases in the domestic money supply, here and elsewhere, occasioned by the effort of central banks to cope with past increases in the US money supply, and relatively fixed, or too slowly adjusting, relationships between the currencies of Western countries.

Having said all of this, it remains that a substantial part of Canada's inflation, and that in most Western countries, is brought about by domestic forces. These forces consist, quite simply, of the competition by those in a strong bargaining position – the corporations and the powerful unions – for larger shares of the increases in the gross national product. I recognize that this competition may be occasioned by a desire to protect real incomes, be they wages or profits, from the erosion that arises from externally induced inflation or indeed any inflation, or by a genuine belief that income shares should be increased for the purpose of remedying wage inequities or of maintaining long-run profit levels. Whatever the reason, the fact remains that so long as there are economic units which are able to protect their real incomes when others are not, or are able to increase their relative share of increases in incomes by more than their increase in productivity when others are not, prices will rise. For it is by price increases that these relative increases in the incomes of those in Galbraith's planning system are realized and by which the cost is passed on to others. The whole process can be self-defeating, of course, if most of the economic units are in the planning system and few are in the market system. But it remains that inflation is the result.

And it remains that macro-economic policy, demand management, the new economics – however you want to describe fiscal and monetary and balance-of-payments policies – is unable by itself to cope with these forces. The reason is not hard to find. If society subscribed to only one value – stable price levels and the growth presumed to be the product of such an economic state – then macro-economics would have the solution: reduce demand, which ultimately is to say increase unemployment, to the point where firms become fearful of raising their prices to validate profit increases or higher wage settlements.

Society, however, has other values which render this prescription unacceptable. Canadians and others no longer are prepared to tolerate the extreme hardships which arise from drastic reductions in family income arising from unemployment, nor do they seem even to believe that unemployment is a preferable state to work, however good periodic doses of slack may be for the economy. They can no longer, in short, stand the sight of demoralizing poverty. To put this metaphorically, unfortunately for the macro-economists, the Judaeo-Christian religion, like a smallpox vaccination, has 'taken.'

Some economists, I should say parenthetically, would argue that the prescription of unemployment to combat inflation was in any event a misinterpretation of Keynes. What he was writing about, and by inference prescribing for, was an economy in which unemployment was rampant, while other economists were insisting, despite all evidence to the contrary, that unemployment would reduce wages, increase profits, increase investment, and thus restore levels of employment. Keynes was not writing about economies in which the state had accepted responsibility for 'high and stable levels of employment.'

That brings me to my second point. It is not only conflicts in values, but with them institutional and behavioural changes in society which have combined to make demand management ineffective – more accurately, unacceptable – as the predominant instrument of economic management. Economic theory, and indeed its application, has not taken adequately into account the great growth in the power of corporations and unions, and their capacity to set and maintain prices and wages despite temporary declines in demand. At some point, of course, this power and this will could be broken by drastic reductions in sales, whether occasioned by very high levels of unemployment or by new and sharp competition. But the norm of institutional behaviour remains: price and wage fixing in large sectors of the economy are administered decisions.

What this means is clear. 'Never mind moderate unemployment and temporary reductions in sales,' say those in a position to set or influence the setting of prices; 'we live in a society where the capacity to set prices and wages will not be broken by excessive reductions in demand. For government has assured us against this contingency, as a result of having accepted as one of its prime responsibilities the maintenance of high and stable levels of employment and income.' This impression is underwritten by governments, indeed, even as they exercise demand management to stabilize prices: they may increase unemployment and reduce income with one hand, but then they return to the unemployed with the other a good two-thirds of the income lost. Governments may even, indeed, create jobs under direct employment programs to put back into employment those whom their demand management policies have put out of work.

I am not deriding politicians, for it is the politicians, not by and large the economists, who came to perceive that the value system of society, combined with the institutional structure of the economy, rendered it impossible to push demand management to the point where it would be fully effective in stabilizing prices. And it was the politicians, too, who perceived that in an economy such as I have described – one in which the dominant elements are more akin to a planning system than a market system – the distribution of income cannot be left to economic forces alone. Hence a social security system designed to achieve a distribution of income more in accord with society's values.

It is enough for me to observe here that economic policy in industrialized nations must increasingly take account of the non-economic forces I have spoken of. It must come to question, if I may speculate a bit, whether the securing of income against inflation can any longer be left to the price and wage fixing process alone. For one reason, this process cannot possibly predict future cost and price increases – if price and wage levels are to be set for any period of time. The result, almost inevitably, is an undershoot or an overshoot in the prices and wages established. For another even more important reason, to leave to the private sector 'planning system' on its own the protection of incomes against inflation is to confer an advantage upon those who function in that system and to leave unprotected those who do not.

It really comes down to this, in short. It matters not whether price or wage increases are designed to protect real incomes in the face of inflation or to remedy some perceived inequity in price or wage relationships: so long as any person's share of real income is increased by raising prices, it must be understood that someone else is being forced to pay for that increased share through the higher prices.

There is, may I say, an optimistic side to this proposition as well as a pessimistic one. The pessimistic one is the argument that the powerful corporations and unions will continue to seek to increase their income shares even when they know that someone less fortunate than they will be forced to pay for these increases. The logical end to this proposition, of course, is either inflation, or price controls, or some attempt to break the bargaining power of corporations and unions.

The optimistic side, however, is this. Recall that it was a sense of justice and compassion which caused governments to underwrite employment and income in the first place. And it was this act of policy, in turn, which dulled the fears of corporations and unions that the increases in prices needed to pay for higher profits or wages would be prevented by sharp declines in income and employment brought on by macro-economic policy. Is it too much to hope that this same sense of justice and compassion might be counted upon, or galvanized, or employed as an instrument of policy, to *restrain* untrammelled competition for income shares? If it came fully to be recognized and were indeed made known that the increases in income shares which have to be financed by price increases must be paid for by others – others who may well be less fortunate than those whose incomes have been increased – would the behaviour of the offending actors in the planning system be influenced?

This is something to be pondered upon, I suggest, however naïve it may sound: the simple proposition that, given community values, widespread information about the consequences of institutional behaviour might itself affect that institutional behaviour in desirable directions.

With this simple proposition I am inclined to put my analysis at rest. Perhaps I might add only this: the imperatives for recognizing the forces which lie behind inflation, and for developing new theories of and policies for income distribution, will be reinforced by the unfolding of the other great issues of which I have spoken. Whether it be to feed the hungry of the world, or to transfer to them some of our growth, or to pay for higher resource costs, or to control pollution, the developed countries of the world can surely expect declining rates of increase in their growth and in their incomes. And as this occurs, the disparities in income in our country will become more apparent, as those with the lowest incomes come no longer to be able to count upon a rapidly growing GNP to improve their absolute well-being.

SOME CONCLUDING GENERALIZATIONS

I would not claim for anything I have said in this paper any great qualities of originality or analytical insight. All I have sought to do is to speak of economics and economic policy in the perspective of the future. But let me conclude with a few generalizations.

My first generalization is this. There is to be observed in all of the issues I have spoken of a certain congruency, in economic terms. It is evident that all of them involve a ranging of other values alongside the traditional economic values of the western world, and that these values can be realized only at some expense to the value of economic growth and material well-being. All of the issues involve, too, institutional forces which, because they are concerned with these competing values, are similarly inimical to continued high rates of growth in the industrialized nations. And all of them lead in the direction of a redistribution of income – both between the rich and the poor nations of the world and within individual nations in the developed world. All of these forces, in short, tend in the direction of lower rates of economic growth for industrialized nations.

True, there will undoubtedly come into play countervailing forces: a greater emphasis on 'benign' technology to maintain industrial production; pressures to 'use' capital rather than 'consume' it, as Boulding would put it; pressures for compensatory growth in the production of services instead of goods; the search for increases in productivity through non-capital improvements; and, internationally, pressures for modes of growth more consistent with labour-intensive societies. But the adjustments will take time, and even when made, they will not likely result in growth rates as high as those to which we have become accustomed.

Finally, there is to be perceived in all of the problems we have examined another common characteristic: their resolution will not be accomplished by market forces or market decisions. In every case administered or planning decisions are called for, whether it be the decision to produce more food, or to control population growth, or to control pollution, or to transfer economic growth, or to distribute income more in harmony with community values.

If this is so, if there is this congruence in these global issues, what does it mean to the economist? It means, it seems to me, as I have tried tentatively to say, that the economist's model must be incorporated into some larger social sciences model – a model which comprehends multiple values, multiple modes of analysis, and multiple methods of making decisions. I suppose in a way I am saying nothing more than that the economist must become multi-disciplinary in his approach; that he must come to recognize with some greater humility than has sometimes been his wont the contribution that the so-called softer disciplines can make to socio-economic analyses.

But in another way I am trying to say more. I put the proposition that the economist's great contributions to building dynamic, quantified, and predictive models ought to be extended to the building, along with other social scientists, of dynamic explanatory models covering the whole range of social, political, and economic decisions. This is not an original proposition, perhaps, but it bears reflecting upon. It has the virtue, it seems to me, of diverting the economist from the attempt to comprehend the world *within* his economic models, and thus from the danger of discarding as externalities anything that doesn't fit. And it has the further virtue of diverting him from his preoccupation with the quantifiable and predictive properties of his models, in favour of encompassing more, if less measurable, variables. What, after all, is so wrong with a dynamic explanatory model, if it at least comprehends the major issues, the major institutional and behavioural forces, and the other pre-eminent if non-quantifiable variables?

The other side of this proposition, of course, is that the economist must concern himself more with decision-making as it occurs outside of his economic model. No one will argue any longer, I should think, that utility maximization by individuals and profit maximization by firms can be said to provide a full explanation for all individual and business decisions. This is all the more the case when the more intangible values, such as compassion and equity and the quality of life, come to be involved. It is possible, of course, to attempt to force decisions based on these values into the economist's model: to include them in our social indifference curves in the form of 'moral satisfaction,' 'self-esteem,' and 'acceptance in the community.' But to do this is surely to distort these values into a form of personal or corporate self-gratification, and thus to lose their real meaning.

The other reason for the economist to place his model into the context of a larger social science model is that decisions made on the basis of non-economic values are in any event taken outside the market system. They are made through the community, whether it be through the political process or some voluntary or co-operative endeavour. So they cannot be comprehended in the economist's model, no matter how he may try. It was in recognition of this fact, as well as the fact of planning decisions in the private sector, that the economists were brought to study decision-making in government and in bureaucracies generally. But in so doing they have, or so it seems to me, sought to replicate in their analyses the market system with which they are familiar. In the process the real essence of decision-making in government – the weighing and balancing of values – has tended to be lost in the economist's art.

Decision-making in the planning system, in short, does not resemble that of the market system, and it calls, therefore, for different modes of analysis. In fact, in the political process, choices between values, or choices between alternative solutions to problems, involve choosing between the *advocates* of the alternatives. From the perspective of the public this involves the conferring of power on leaders who will make the ultimate choices and formulate the ultimate solutions; from the perspective of the advocates of alternative solutions it involves the quest for power – power to act on behalf of the community as a whole.

What is being allocated in the planning system, in other words, is power. What must be examined, therefore, are the concepts of political and sociological theory – such concepts, or forces, as power, authority, legitimacy, and influence. And what must be analysed are the social and political institutions within which these forces are at work and the interplay of the forces themselves. One would naturally expect that this analysis would call upon the disciplines which have concerned themselves for so long with these forces – the political scientist, the legal theorist, the sociologist, even the philosopher. What is equally to the point, the economist could not in any event be expected – in placing his model in this larger context – to take on the whole of the job of social analysis.

The economic outcome, to put this second generalization in other terms, is the outcome of at least two processes: the one the allocation of resources and products; the other the disposition of power. And the two processes interact. Only by putting the models of the social scientists together, and by examining the allocative mechanisms of both of these processes, will we succeed, it seems to me, in developing the perspectives which are so essential to a comprehensive analysis of the global problems which confront us.

Let me say something, finally, as a third and concluding generalization, about public policy decision-making. Traditional modes of decision-making in government have tended toward the development of solutions to problems as they arose. They have not generally taken the form of forward planning, of identifying potential problems and placing them in a comprehensive framework, or of prescribing objectives and developing co-ordinated directions of policy to achieve them. Rather public policy formulation has tended to take the form, to use a government expression, of 'ad hocery.'

This has always been a hazardous approach to decision-making. It assumes that the problem will not reach such alarming proportions as to call for draconian solutions. And it assumes that the risks of miscalculation are relatively small, since the consequences of miscalculation have always been relatively small, whether in the form of unrest or rebellion or even war. And this, in a sense, has been true. For governments, at least Western governments, always had available to them a pervasively powerful weapon: whether to solve the problems as they arose or to meet the consequences of miscalculations in resolving them. That weapon was economic growth. Recall only how it has been used to ameliorate poverty, and therefore social unrest, while at the same time preserving existing patterns of income distribution. And recall how economic growth has been used to enervate the causes, or to ameliorate the consequences, of international conflict.

One is forced to question, however, whether all this is changing. The problems which loom on the horizon are surely larger than those of the past. They are global rather than regional or national in character. They are capable of burgeoning beyond the capability of conventional solutions. And the hazards of miscalculation, whether in the timing or the adequacy of the solutions, are manifestly greater in an atomic age than before. What is equally discomforting is the gnawing doubt that the world has enough economic growth to go around for the early enough amelioration of the problem it confronts.

What does this mean for the political process? It means, surely, that those who assume public responsibility increasingly will be assuming the burden of trying to perceive the big decisions, rather than waiting for them to emerge; that they will have to take more of a lead in solving the problems rather than waiting for some political imperative to force the solutions upon them.

This is no easy matter, if my analysis of the grand issues is at all valid. For each of them calls for the leaders of the industrialized world to distribute, in some measure, the burdens of less growth rather than the benefits of more. Some analysts are sceptical about leaders in a democracy being able to persuade the public to accept such adjustments: they predict, in effect, that authoritarianism is required in times of adversity.[12] I suspect this is true, if one assumes that the public cannot be persuaded to accept the causes of slower growth as 'causes' – as *their* objectives or aims – as well as recognizing them simply as explanatory events. People in positions of public responsibility will, in short, have to lead rather more than they follow, to proselytize rather than simply to respond to public pressure. And we as citizens will have to come to accept this kind of leadership as something more than mere moralizing.

The consequences for government itself are similarly sobering, I suspect. Decisions between values, or the interposition into social decisions of values other than purely economic ones, are largely made by governments. Traditionally this has meant more government and larger government, taking the form sometimes of the provision of services and sometimes of regulatory requirements. The sheer scale of government required to make and to give effect to these choices between values may just as surely lead to a form of authoritarianism, it can be argued with force, as the need to bring about public acceptance of the choices involved. And what is the remedy for that?

Again I am unable to prescribe. But I suspect that the solution lies in the direction of greater public-private partnership: of governments postulating general 'policy principles,' and of the private sector, business and personal, accepting these principles as ground rules, just as they presently accept economic forces as ground rules. The alternatives – an ever-expanding government bureaucracy to give effect to non-economic choices, or an ever-expanding uncertainty generated by rule-making tribunals designed to bring the private sector to do the right thing – are scarcely reassuring.

My concluding generalization, in short, is that the private sector, both corporate and individual, organized and unorganized, must bring itself to recognize the major issues which confront the world; it must itself recognize the consequences for them of resolving these issues; and it must itself embrace new ground rules for corporate and individual behaviour which will give effect to the choices which have to be made.

NOTES

1 'The second crisis of economic theory,' *American Economic Review*, May 1972, p. 10
2 'Today's apocalypses and yesterday's,' *ibid.*, May 1973, p. 110
3 K. E. Boulding, 'Income or welfare,' *Review of Economic Studies*, 1949-1950 issue, p. 82
4 'The second crisis of economic theory,' p. 8
5 Jay W. Forrester, *World Dynamics* (Cambridge, Mass., 1971); D. H. Meadows *et al.*, *The Limits to Growth* (New York, 1972); Robert L. Heilbroner, *An Inquiry into the Human Prospect* (New York, 1974)
6 Shirley Foster Hartley, *Population Quantity vs Quality* (Englewood Cliffs, NJ, 1972), p. 154
7 John Kenneth Galbraith, *Economics and the Public Purpose* (Boston, 1973)
8 This analysis was made by Farmanfarmian, Gutowski, Okita, Roosa, and Wilson in 'How can the world afford OPEC oil?,' *Foreign Affairs*, Jan. 1975
9 G. Evelyn Hutchison, 'The biosphere,' *Scientific American*, Sept. 1970, p. 53
10 'A little more time,' *Economist*, 29 June 1974, p. 15. The quotation refers to Wilfrid Beckerman's criticisms of the environmentalists.
11 *New York Times*, 5 Jan. 1975
12 See Heilbroner, *An Inquiry into the Human Prospect*

The abyss of authoritarianism

CHARLES TAYLOR

The politics of the steady state

In pondering the political possibilities and impossibilities of the steady state, we do not need to accept any of the predictions of disaster put forward recently concerning the future of mankind (although any one of these gloomy predictions may easily be close to the truth). We only have to accept the proposition that our present patterns of exponential growth in population and industrial development must somewhere hit against limits of three kinds:

a population limit beyond which the supply of basic necessities, especially food, cannot be assured for larger numbers;

a resource limit, where the supply of non-renewable resources is so reduced as first to make increasing consumption impossible and later to force us to do without altogether;

a pollution limit, whereby the ecologically harmful side effects of increased production become a danger to life.

There may also be other limits, such as a population-concentration limit, which may already have been reached in large conurbations today, well before the limit of food supply mentioned above. The close-packed concentration of tens of millions of human beings leads beyond a certain point to individual and social breakdown, expressed in 'anomic' violence, increasing mutual mistrust and hostility, more and more frenetic attempts to escape society by privatization, and perhaps other as yet unknown terrors.

But this latter limit is speculative, in the sense that there are indications but no solid evidence for it; and the exact shape of the three undeniable limits is very much a matter of dispute. For those who, like the authors of the *The Limits to Growth*, are willing to put some kind of time span on our progress towards the limits there are always objectors who point to the possibilities of avoiding or pushing back the limits. For instance, if one of the big barriers we now threaten to run against is thermal pollution – that is, the addition to the earth's heat from the sun by internal sources of man-made heat through the burning of fossil fuels or the transforming of other kinds of energy (hydro-electric generation), thereby at some (unknown) point producing disastrous climatic changes – we can always hope that the switch to solar energy will allow us to meet all our growing energy needs from the sun's existing flows of heat.

The layman rapidly loses his way in these disputes and becomes incapable of arbitrating. And in this area we are all partly laymen, since the range of expertise and scientific knowledge required straddles so many fields that no one person can master them all. But however difficult it is to predict the detail, when we step back from these disputes we can surely see in general outline what the requirements must be for future human society. They spell the end of exponential quantitative growth.

For setting aside the cases where the ways around the limits proposed by the 'optimists' themselves have other unacceptable side-effects (e.g., energy through hydrogen fusion, which solves the problem of scarce resources but not at all those of thermal or other forms of pollution), the new ways can, no more than the old, open the way to unlimited exponential growth. For instance, the potential of solar and geothermal energy may be so large as to be, for our purposes, unlimited. But tapping these sources requires investment, and tapping them in ever-increasing amounts requires ever-larger investment and hence increasing use of other resources. Thus tapping solar heat for power purposes requires giving over some (at present quite large) parts of the earth's surface to reflectors, and this area obviously couldn't be increased beyond a certain point without hampering other essential uses or provoking harmful ecological effects.

The crude layman's intuition is that with so large and varied a number of limits awaiting us somewhere out there on our trajectory of exponential growth, our chances of missing *all* of them, by some dazzling manoeuvre worthy of a comic strip hero, are just about nil. It seems overwhelmingly likely that as we swerve our star-ship to avoid one we will charge into another. For the range of such limits is much wider and more multiform than the above neat three-fold classification suggests. There are many possible scenarios in which the world may run into the hunger barrier, and there are a large number of essential resources which may run out. Above all, there is an indefinite number of lethal pollution effects or ecologically disastrous consequences of increased production. It is quite possible that the most lethal are as yet unknown to us. The scenario of a world rendered uninhabitable by human agency through a completely unforeseen chain of effects, dear to science fiction authors, is far from implausible. The wild optimists, the Buck Rogers of our growth Odyssey, are dreaming of that sublime technological coup, the invention of the perfect gimmick, which infinitely increases potency without cost, satirized by Al Capp in the Valley of the Schmoon.

Sooner or later, we shall all have to live within economic systems which respect certain limits: 1/ a stable population; 2/ a severe rationing of non-renewable resources, the stock of which must ultimately sink to what can be recycled perpetually; 3/ a ban on the increase of certain side-effects of production, such as the creation of heat or the emission of certain substances into soil, water, or atmosphere, so that any increase in production must be accompanied by more effective counter-action, such as the recycling of waste substances.

It might be thought that this reflection is too general. It applies to the world as a whole, but all this is going to hit the different countries and parts of the world at very different rates and times, and in very different ways. Population limit is a reality in Bangladesh but surely not in Canada, we might argue, with its immense spaces and sparse population. A similar point might be made about resource exhaustion, again considering our exceptional endowment. But quite apart from humanitarian considerations, this may be a very foolish line of thought. We are a relatively weak country, small in industrial and military might. The world may not let us go on enjoying our incredible advantage in natural endowment and go on living in the old pattern of unrestrained growth, while everyone else is forced into the new straitened mould. And besides this, a relatively generous endowment in space and resources doesn't free us from all of the multiform limits that we face. There are numerous pollution effects to which we are heir along with all other peoples (indeed, many pollution effects are more serious in the North, where lie large parts of our 'great open spaces'). Or again, we may not have reached the population limit in the sense that our food supply is inadequate; but if there is a population concentration limit, we may soon, in our large cities, be hitting the point at which the quality of social life rapidly deteriorates.

Hence we too will have one day to start thinking in terms of the steady state society, which we might define first as one which respects the three limits just mentioned. And for this we are grievously unprepared: respecting these limits means renouncing expotential quantitative growth.

Respecting the three limits doesn't mean that all growth is impossible. For there are qualitative changes which we understand as growth because we consider the end-result more valuable, even though they involve no greater use of material resources. Let us say that a firm improves the quality of the wallpaper it produces by improving its design, and this improvement consists entirely in a more aesthetically pleasing pattern, the actual use of materials being the same. This in some sense is growth in that people now have higher quality decoration in their houses. And it could even be measured as such in the gross national product

(GNP), since we can imagine that the firm would charge more for this superior product.

Thus it is possible to increase the quantities of certain products by better design or by eliminating waste without needing increased resources as, for example, when a handy man builds a solar heater for his house out of waste products, or when we revert to an older design of clothes-peg which doesn't require the metal clasp.

These forms of growth, what we might call quality growth and greater economy, remain possible even in the most stringently resource-pressed society. But what will be ruled out is long runs of continuing quantitative increases in production. Of course, not all resources will be limited: renewable ones and those of such great abundance that we need never worry will be there for the asking. But the expanding exploitation of these resources will require at some point either the increased use of non-renewable resources or will increase some pollution effect. To continue on the path of increased production will thus require greater efforts at counteraction, thus increasing costs. And since it is frequently the case (exemplified in *Limits to Growth*, p. 142, in the matter of reducing organic wastes from a beet sugar plant) that pollution control involves steeply mounting costs as its aims for more complete effectiveness, the increase in costs will be exponential.

The steady state society will thus allow for qualitative growth, for all growths in quantity due to new designs which are more economical in resource use, and for short runs of quantitative growth which make use of renewable or astronomically abundant resources (e.g., hydrogen) which can surge forward until they hit a limit in their use of non-renewable resources or in their pollution effects. But what would be impossible would be continuing exponential quantitative growth, where the production of one phase is the base from which the increased output of the next phase is generated by some continuing percentage of growth. And to rule this out is to rule out exponential growth altogether, since exponential qualitative growth is a meaningless category.

Of course, this notion of a steady state society is an idealization. It may be that we will never be all that strapped. Or – and this is, alas, more likely – it may be that we will be more catastrophically deprived, as we overshoot, run out of some essential resource, and have to cut everything back (a foretaste of which we came close to experiencing in the recent oil crisis). But to take the optimistic side, we will probably always have *some* non-renewable resources that we can still afford to be prodigal about; and there will always be *some* pollution effects which we can afford to be reckless about for a while. These will certainly lengthen our bursts of quantitative growth. But the steady state society must define the asymptote towards which we shall be inexorably forced to move.

We are lamentably unprepared for this steady state society. And this is because we are wedded to exponential growth. Exponential growth is measured, conceived, worried about, and celebrated in our societies by the figure for GNP. This is expected to grow each year by some hefty and sustained percentage. Much has been written of this almost ridiculous obsession with the GNP, this idolatry of growth. But it is not just a weakness in the head of politicians, journalists, and academics (though all of these groups may be weak enough in the head); it is much more deeply rooted in our society, in its definitions of hope, the future, the good life – indeed in the very way in which we are integrated as a society.

Let us try to enumerate the ways in which exponential growth is essential to us. This is not an easy task, for some ways are hard to define, but the attempt I will make here will be enough to show how deep and wide it cuts.

1 Our society counts on continued growth to maintain full employment. This has been a feature of all 'capitalist' societies. Any serious drop in the rate of growth of GNP means stagnation, widespread unemployment, and distress, often very unfairly distributed with a much heavier incidence in the poor, underdeveloped regions.

2 Our society relies on growth to meet one of the most pressing demands made on it, that for a just and more equal distribution of benefits. Modern societies, having swept aside any of the previous ontological justifications for hierarchy or differential life predicaments, are faced with a continuing demand for the equalization of life chances. The surviving justifications for unequal distribution, based on merit, supposed contribution to society, or effort, are either becoming more transparently unacceptable (how can one estimate the value of *individual* effort, when the most productive enterprises of modern society are vast, interdependent, collective achievements?), or else fail to justify the existing degree and type of inequality (how can differences of merit justify hereditary structural disabilities, such as affect people in underprivileged regions and classes?).

Faced with the demand for greater equality, which our society in its own terms cannot gainsay, and therefore which is pressed more and more urgently and imperiously by those who feel themselves disadvantaged, our response has been to pin everything on growth. In a static economy, greater equality would mean redistribution, which would mean lowering the living standard of the better off to raise that of the poorer. But this is all the more unthinkable in our society in that the very definition of happiness and the good life in a technological civilization includes the progressive increase in prosperity over the life-cycle, and prosperity in turn is defined by the increased command over goods and services. To face our affluent classes with not only a standstill in income growth but an actual cut-back would be adding the unbelievable to the unacceptable. Static redistribution is hard to achieve, if not impossible, in any society; but in ours doubly so.

And so the only way that we can see to cope with the strains of inequality is to treat it with the spin-off effects of growth. The minimal or right-wing hope is that people on steadily rising incomes will not care too much that income disparities are remaining constant or even getting worse – in other words that others are getting richer. The maximal, or left-wing, hope is that a disproportionate share of growth can be steered to the less well-off so that income disparities can be reduced, but painlessly, since this time the rich are compensated (or anaesthetized) by rising incomes for the more rapid progress of the poor.

As a matter of fact, this latter hope has been cruelly disappointed both internationally and domestically in most industrial countries. This seems to happen both because of the very mechanisms of exponential growth and because of the expectation of increased incomes mentioned above. An economy grows exponentially because the production of one year is the base for the increased production the following year by some non-secularly declining percentage of growth. But in real terms this means, of course, that most of the growth will happen where it has already happened. Thus world growth sees the industrialized nations pulling ahead of the underdeveloped ones by more and more frightening margins. And something similar tends to happen between regions in Canada, although it is to some extent offset by transfer payments, and government attempts at encouraging development.

At the same time, the affluent refuse to behave according to the left-wing scenario and not to mind or notice when a disproportionately high share of growth goes to the disadvantaged. The laws of exponential growth seem to hold in regard to expectations as well, and in our richer times we hear more gnashing of teeth about (non-corporate) welfare bums, more churlish resentment at any attempt at relative redistribution than in previous decades. The very ideology of growth, the very celebration of its benefits, seems to pre-empt its product through the rising demands of the powerful and affluent, so that mountains of munitions are piled up for a war on poverty which never begins.

But the failure of the egalitarian hope makes our reliance on growth all the more urgent and unavoidable. If greater equality evades us, then only rapid all-around growth can compensate the disadvantaged for their unjust plight (we hope). Affluent western economies may come to resemble rich men in the grip of a blackmailer; they will have to pay higher and higher sums to keep things quiet. And paying higher and higher sums means maintaining exponential growth.

3   This expectation of an endless increase in prosperity, which in the past has countered egalitarian hopes, can itself be seen as an independent form of addiction to exponential growth, since it would make the steady state very hard to bear for us even if we had no redistributional imperative. But it is hard to define this addiction and even harder to get to its roots. We can see it as defining the

good life to include an ever-increasing command over goods and services, and an ever-increasing capacity to control nature for individual ends. This definition of the good life would, of course, have seemed wicked if not incomprehensible to men of many previous epochs. But it seems to be very deeply rooted in our own. And as long as this is so, our adjustment to the steady state will be very difficult and painful.

What then are the roots of this addiction? In part, they lie in the sense, widespread in modern civilization, of what it is to be a human being: control over nature, the shaping of things to our freely chosen projects, with the attendant definition of autonomy as self-dependence, and the focus on the future, are of paramount importance. This, which has sometimes been referred to as 'the modern identity,' is very difficult to define exactly, especially in the narrow compass of this talk. But it should be listed as an independent mode of addiction to growth, because it operates in any modern technological society, even one where the increase in *individual* prosperity counted for nothing as in the ideal 'socialist' society (are there any such? perhaps China – for the present; certainly not the nations of the Soviet bloc). For these societies too would measure their success and their worth by production, by the steady increase of mastery over nature – in short by growth. A steady state society, on the other hand, requires that we accept, and hence come to value, a balance of some kind with our surroundings, one that will perhaps be constantly undergoing micro-reorderings from within as we strive for qualitative growth, but which will no longer offer the prospect of a linear increase in potency, let alone an exponential one.

The importance of this modern productive identity is also visible in our nonsocialist societies in many other ways than just the expectation of rising prosperity. We too celebrate our collective triumphs over nature, such as the moon landing. We measure the health of our society by the rate of growth of GNP; we justify it as a producing society. And more important, this justifying image of ourselves as a vast interdependent enterprise of production is part of the essential rationale for social differentiation, one of the main underpinnings of social discipline, one of the things that holds our society together.

Indeed, we are very aware of this now, because this justifying image is weakening its hold on our minds, along with a weakening of the modern identity among a substantial part of the rising generation; partly as a result, we find that the disciplines and restraints on which we counted in the past are slipping. Contemporary industrial societies appear, more than in the immediately preceding decades, to be cockpits of struggle between groups seeking an acceptable level of income, privilege, or dignity, becoming more and more determined to achieve their objectives, and more indignant when they do not, and being less willing to compromise and restrain themselves in the name of supposed over-riding social goods.

But if the modern identity and its attendant sense of common social purpose is already slipping in this period of unprecedented growth, how will we accommodate to the steady state? It seems that we are committed to growth through the very underpinnings of our industrial society.

This brings us to our principal problem – the politics of the steady state. For the deeply disturbing prospect which arises from this list of our commitments to growth is that our present reasonably free, reasonably democratic, reasonably civilized polities might be casualties of the enforced shift to the steady state. If we can barely meet the demand for fairer shares through breakneck growth, how can we cope when growth is dramatically reduced and ceases to be exponential? Our society will fly apart.

Of course, 'fly apart' is a metaphor. Societies rarely fly apart. What happens when they cease to be able to hold together through a traditional set of institutions is that they mutate to another set in which force, violence, and coercion have a greater role. There is a coup, an army or police take-over; or great masses of citizens tacitly consent when a government destroys traditional liberties and takes dictatorial power.

The first *raison-d'être* for growth, that we count on it to maintain full employment, is not decisive. For the switch to a steady state would in fact call for a great effort, would force us to reintroduce labour-intensive technologies in some cases, and require a very important productive drive to retool us for the change; for instance, immense investment would be required in recycling technology and equipment, anti-pollution devices, and the like. The impact of scarcity, provided we are capable of any organized response at all, will require an immense redirection of our productive effort, comparable to wartime. Unless our economy collapses into chaos, and we allow progressive shortages just to disorganize production without any effort to reshape our economy, we should suffer no more than severe transitional unemployment (which may be bad enough, but not the same as another depression).

But the second and third rationales for growth addiction are of decisive importance. Our society, in which the good life is defined partly in terms of ever-increasing prosperity (that is, individual command over goods and services) and in which differences of income, privilege, and life-chance become progressively less justifiable while they remain intractably undiminished, is already under severe strain. The strain is increased, as we saw, by the weakening of one of its most important justifying self-images, that of a society of interdependent producers. There seems to be an internal dynamic in this kind of society in which individuals and groups feel justified in pressing increasing demands both in the name of equality and under their entitlement to ever-increasing prosperity. These demands are pressed more imperiously and often truculently, and less willingness to compromise or to heed appeals (spurious or genuine) in the name of the general welfare.

One of the more benign, or less malignant, manifestations of this growing free-for-all is the income scramble, which is part cause in almost all advanced industrial economies of the increasing rate of price inflation. But there are other, more terrifying forms. Members of some disadvantaged groups have resorted sporadically to terrorism. Admittedly, this happens where the issue is not just differences of income and privilege, but rather as part of a systematic denial of dignity and freedom to the group in question. But it would be wrong to see these two kinds of struggle, the utilitarian income scramble and the terroristic demand for rights, as necessarily two qualitatively different things, separated by water-tight compartments. Who has not heard these days the demand for higher incomes and more equality framed in the rhetoric of rights and liberation?

Still, it would take something to bring a society over the leap from the mere income scramble such as we see in contemporary Britain to the terrorist war of desperate minorities such as we see in Northern Ireland (and now spilling over to Britain). But the kind of shock that might do it would be just such a forced, rapid transition to the steady state. In a society in which groups are intent on increasing their members' prosperity, and on at least maintaining their present rate of growth and sometimes increasing it, where this determination is fuelled by the widespread acceptance of the consumer-goods standard of happiness, what happens when growth must be slowed down? Income growth has to be halted, privileged groups become ever more determined to resist redistribution at all costs, disadvantaged groups become more desperate and combative, less willing to accept appeals to general social solidarity. At the same time everyone suffers the frustration of controls, for a society of increasingly scarce resources is one that requires rationing and restrictions. This cuts across one of the key features of individual prosperity as commonly understood, that in his increasing command over consumer goods the individual exercises increasing choice.

A crisis of this kind could possibly produce a mutation, a sudden rediscovery of social solidarity and common purpose, as did the evacuation from Dunkirk by Britain during the last war. I want to turn to explore what would be involved in this kind of transformation in a moment. But the frightening scenario I am considering here is that the society may face the crisis without any such regeneration. And here the prospect is of an increasing bitterness and desperation in the intergroup struggle, a greater and greater willingness to hold society to ransom by whatever means available, which may extend all the way to the means of violence. Terrorism only requires the action of small minorities; from the majority of a given group it only demands a certain moral ambivalence, sufficient to avoid active collaboration with the forces of order, as in the situation existing in the Catholic ghettos of Ulster.

A society terrorized would 'fly apart.' Sooner or later, the majority of citizens, who only identify sporadically with the desperadoes, will be willing to abdicate

whatever power they possess as an electorate and many of their traditional free-
doms to a strong-arm government which will restore order. This change may not
come in as spectacular, bloody, and revolting a way as the army coup in Chile
(where society seems to have 'flown apart' for other reasons than those considered here); perhaps the Uruguayan case should be a more worrying precedent,
where the power of democratic institutions can be slowly undermined with the
tacit consent of a citizenry who have been through an extended experience of
terrorism.

In this scenario either overt dictatorship or a society substantially more under
authoritarian direction and control becomes the only 'solution,' the only way of
imposing the necessary restrictions, the only way to impose *some* sharing of the
social product which the groups cannot acquiesce to through free bargaining or
accept out of social solidarity.

The question of the politics of the steady state can thus be more precisely put in
this way: is there any way of avoiding this authoritarian scenario? Is there another way of meeting the transition to the steady state and the challenges of
adjustment, by which we can preserve and perhaps even extend our liberties, our
democratic institutions, and the level of civilized behaviour we have attained in
our public life? Of course, a crucial part of what makes the difference, of what
provokes, for instance, a Dunkirk spirit or its opposite, can never be adequately
defined. But perhaps something can be said of the changes in institutions and
publically accepted goals which would be part of a more creative and civilized
political response to the steady state.

The ensuing reflections are fragmentary and abstract but, fortunately, not entirely general. The focus of my questioning, sometimes unstated, sometimes
stated, will be this country and its possibilities. The passages of general discussion
of societies in the steady state are preparatory to putting a question about a
particular society. If someone from another country were to engage in a general
discussion about the steady state, he would probably focus on quite different
things. There is no doubt an implied criticism here of my general considerations,
but I don't know how to make them more genuinely universal without losing my
bearings altogether.

Perhaps the place to start would be to ask how a steady state society can meet
the demand for greater equality without lapsing into an authoritarian pattern. I
think an essential condition of this would be the elaboration, partly by spontaneous convergence, partly by design, of a normal pattern of consumption
which was accessible to the least affluent.

The major challenge to a steady state society comes as we saw from the fact
that our present pattern of inequality is basically intolerable and is made pro-

visionally tolerable only by rapid growth. But there are different patterns of inequality, and not all of them are equally intolerable or intolerable in the same way. There is, for instance, the inequality between the mass of the population on one hand and a handful of spectacularly privileged on the other. In certain circumstances this is felt by the majority to be absolutely unacceptable; for instance, where the minority enjoy their privileges by directly exploiting the masses, where they are landlords, say, and the majority are their rack-rented tenants; or where, even without exploitation, the life of the majority is felt as intolerable in itself, quite apart from any comparison; or where the privileged are exempt from certain necessary disciplines and sacrifices imposed on everyone else (e.g., they are evading taxation on a lavish scale like many American political leaders).

Outside these circumstances, however, this kind of inequality frequently does not evoke resentment or indignation. Multi-millionaires have generally not been resented in North American society, as the remains of a leisured aristocracy are generally not in Europe. No one is enraged when Howard Hughes rents himself a Central American republic, or Countess So-and-So marries into some dispossessed royal family. For this kind of behaviour has nothing to do with normal life. Not to be like that is not a deprivation for the great majority, even though many in fantasy may imagine themselves with the wealth and leverage of Howard Hughes.

Or again, there are societies with a deeply entrenched class division, where the classes have their different respective modes of life. This was the case in medieval and early modern Europe, as indeed it was in almost all large and complex societies until the last century or so. In this kind of society there are a number of different models of normal life, and although these differ in the wealth that men have at their disposal or in their ability to wield power or display themselves, these differences may not be resented by those less privileged because these capacities of wealth, power, and display are not part of *their* normal life.

What is intolerable about the inequality in a contemporary industrial society is that these societies have developed a single norm of acceptable life, but this norm is accessible only to about 60 to 75 per cent of the population. The non-affluent minority, a quarter to two-fifths of the population, are in a totally unacceptable position; they are unable to live by a standard which is defined universally as *the* normal standard of a decent life. And this standard becomes increasingly inescapable as modern societies dissolve and sweep away in their normal course of evolution all differentiated and heterogeneous sub-cultures; as mobility loosens the ties of regional and historic communities, as the pervasive single communications network penetrates deeper into everyone's life, as growth sweeps away older landmarks, and as the ideology of a producing society draws people away from their allegiance to the past and towards the future of increasing mastery over things.

This is not to say that another kind of diversity doesn't spring up, one of tastes, styles, avocations, even sexual mores, personal discipline. But this diversity is very fragile; people are not deeply anchored in their options of style or even sexual mores, as they were in regional and historical communities. And this diversity has an underlying common premise, that individuals *choose* among these different styles and mores, and they can choose because they have some minimum command as individuals over the shape of their lives, and they get this in our society by being consumers at or above a certain standard of living. Of course, there are objectors who want to reject this latter equation, who dream of and even may try to create a counter-society in which men can be individually free in a communitarian context in balance with nature. But this minority has been quite ineffective in actually creating an alternative (although its criticism has had a deep echo in the structure of our society and has contributed to its failure of nerve). And as has often been pointed out, this minority comes to a large degree from those who have already 'made it' on the consumer standard, and very frequently have a super-standard life to fall back on if things go wrong.

In our society the affluent three-fifths can hope to enjoy such things as a reasonably secure and non-demeaning job, decent housing, the full range of consumer durables, a holiday away from time to time (either travel or cottage), some chance for further education for their children. The rest face the grim prospect of missing out on these. And this is made absolutely intolerable by the fact that such possessions and possibilities are defined as the normal decent life. In part this is a function of the fact that the majority now enjoy them (even though it may be a bare majority). People with memories stretching back far enough have often remarked that even greater deprivation was in a way more bearable during the Depression because 'everyone' was then in the same boat. But it is also a creation of our modern society, with its inexorable action of sweeping away partial communities and imposing the single norm which suits the modern identity.

This pattern of inequality is intolerable in a way that the others – that of a deeply class-differentiated society, that of a small minority of spectacularly privileged – are not. This intolerable inequality is one of the major sources of strain, which we are easing temporarily through (at least the promise of) growth. But this pattern could not be sustained in a free society once it had reached the steady state.

A society forced to give up exponential growth, and which responded to this by freezing the existing pattern of distribution, or where necessary, rolling everyone back proportionately, would become a smouldering volcano. It would sooner or later have to abandon some of its free institutions and go over into an authoritarian pattern, with a large, irresponsible apparatus for the maintenance of order. But at the same time a society which responded to the end of exponential growth by trying a radical levelling down would also provoke volcanic discontent. This solution, too, might only be possible under a dictatorship and/or massive emigration of the better-off (as in the case of Cuba under Fidel).

When looked at in this way, the future of freedom looks gloomy indeed. And perhaps this is the most realistic perspective. But being a compulsive optimist, I would like to try to look at it another way. If we set aside for the moment the problem of the transition, where special factors may be in play, as I argue below, and focus on what new pattern of society could be potentially a free society, we can perhaps outline one which, however unlikely, is conceivable.

The kind of society which could be sustained under the stable state would be one in which the consumption standard defining a normal decent life would be available generally speaking, to the most disadvantaged. (I say 'generally speaking' for there will probably always be some special cases of disability or misfortune which the most dedicatedly egalitarian society will not be able to cope with.) I am assuming for the moment a single such standard, because it seems obvious that any attempt to recreate a class-differentiated society, besides being undesirable, would be clearly impossible in a modern, technological, urbanized, communications-saturated civilization. Later on, however, we may lift this assumption to look at the possibility that a new *regional* differentiation may grow (or return), for this would obviously have special relevance for a country like ours.

This kind of standard for 'normal' life, in which there is no one left out below, as it were, exists of itself in some simple and relatively indigent societies. But clearly in our case it would have to be created. At present the normal standard is partly defined by a command over an ever-growing and ever-diversifying range of consumer goods and services, such that it is always economically unfeasible to provide it for everyone. If any range of goods is available for everyone then it cannot exhaust the standard; this is almost a corollary of the ideology of growth. What we would need in the steady state is a redefined, relatively static standard (one which grew only slowly and irregularly) which everyone could feasibly enjoy.

But how could such a thing be brought about? In terms of mechanism by a systematic policy of rationing and subsidies. What is necessary is some consensus about the commonly available standard, what goes to make it up: let us say, beyond a certain food budget, a certain quality of housing, some level of education, health care, availability of personal transport, possibility of travel, and so on. (Need I mention that this standard is utterly different from the minimum standards of welfare or other transfer payments of our present society, which are meant as survival minima and must be set well below the norm of decent living?)

The aim of public policy would be to ensure by a mixture of rationing and subsidy that the goods and services of this common standard are available at prices which everyone can meet (including, of course, zero price in the case of such services as education and health care). In some cases this could be done by allocating resources to producers (i.e., rationing at the producers' level) to ensure that the supply of certain goods is sufficient to keep its price down. In other cases it could be done by subsidy as well. And in some cases, where an essential resource was scarce, it might have to be rationed to the consumer, possibly at controlled prices.

The results of this (or at least the desired result) would be that the goods of the standard would be available to everyone's budget, but that the goods and services outside this range, being relatively starved of resources and unsubsidized, would be much more highly priced. Suppose that the standard includes some utility vehicle for personal transport (whether this is a car or some species of motor-bicycle will depend on how constrained we are for resources, relative pollution levels, and so on). Then some more luxurious vehicle would be spectacularly more expensive, and would in fact be purchased with their excess income by very few. This would not necessarily mean, of course, that there would be a minority of privileged with Cadillacs, expensive dwellings, holidays in Tahiti, and so on. This is a distinct possibility in almost any form of society. Luxuries may in fact be dispersed more widely, as some people find it possible to take a flyer on a Cadillac, others on an expensive house, others again on tours to Tahiti (which might even, in certain fortunate conditions, be part of the standard). What is essential to this pattern of distribution, however, is that the great majority be at or near the standard, so that, if resources increase well beyond what is necessary to maintain it at present levels, the standard should be raised, rather than that the luxury sector be allowed to proliferate and so eventually create a new socially effective standard from which a substantial minority is left out below.

I can hear in advance the groans of my readers as they take in the import of these paragraphs. It looks as though in addition to the dangers of dictatorship I am holding out the prospect of a Byzantine society in which production and consumption are held in a static pattern by a myriad of controls, and in which the pattern of consumption is marked by the drab uniformity of the utility good. The economics of Byzantium combine with the taste of wartime Britain; we see the prospect of an endless diet of Brussels sprouts eaten under the watchful eye of the Eparch of Constantinople.

I can't say that I am unambiguously overjoyed at the prospect myself. But I have two contradictory things to say in partial mitigation: first, that things are going to be that bad anyway whatever we do; and second, that they don't need to be all that bad.

On the first point: we have to face the fact that when we hit the limits of scarce resources and unacceptable pollution levels, we shall *have* to start allocating resources and/or licences to produce. We saw this with the US oil crisis last winter: gas was made more difficult to obtain for the private motorist in order to safeguard supplies for industry and heating. When we come to the limits of growth, this kind of allocation will become the rule rather than the exception. And in cases of great scarcity, we shall have to face consumer rationing as well.

This allocation by public policy will replace a more haphazard system in force today, loosely and misleadingly referred to as 'the market.' In fact, allocations are made today by business decisions, most often of large corporations who are operating within the limits of what they believe they can induce consumers to buy at generally managed prices. This doesn't mean, of course, that they operate in conditions of unlimited freedom; they have to contend on one side with scarcity and the claims of rivals to the same resources, on the other with the not always predictable boundary of consumer interests. But their freedom is that of self-designed growth through shaping demand within these boundaries.

It ought not to be thought a step backward if this system, whose global result is haphazard, but whose partial consequences are determined by private and irresponsible concentrations of power, is replaced by public and responsible decision-making. And this is the more so if we reflect that the thrust of the present system is towards the entrenchment and extension of the consumer goods standard of happiness; for the condition of the growth of corporations is the perpetual extension and diversification of consumer demand. These indeed are the major institutions which embody and sustain with all the power and influence at their command the religion of infinite productive growth, the conception of the good life as ever-increasing individual command over goods and services.

What is legitimately depressing about the prospect of the steady state society is not that the major allocations of resources between priorities will be conscious and public, but rather the perhaps terrible conditions of scarcity under which such choices will be made. It is this which will force us to forgo the endless proliferation of consumer goods. There will just not be enough resources. A freely proliferating consumer bonanza would be a privilege which only a few participated in, and which could in principle never 'trickle down' through the beneficent action of exponential growth. If anyone prefers a recreation of the society of Marie Antoinette to one in which priority is given to a universal standard, I regret I haven't the space here to argue the case in morals and political theory. I want just to make the point that such a society could only be held in that mould by force, and it would most likely end in the same way as its illustrious eighteenth-century analogue.

But to come to the second point: things don't have to be that bad. A society with a universally available consumer standard can still be one in which there is lots of choice, good design, alternative designs, and alternative sources of design. Within the standard 'package' people could obviously choose less consumer durables in order to have more interesting holidays. But beyond this, the goods of the standard, those which benefit from resource allocations or subsidies, don't have to be standardized. What has to be determined is the amount of resources used per unit. A 'utility' frigidaire, for instance, would be defined as one which did not exceed a certain budget of resources in its manufacture. Outside of that there need be no limit other than economic on the variety of designs or the number of firms public, co-operative, or private, doing the designing.

And beyond this we can hope that people might rediscover other ways of expressing and realizing variety and colour than those of the proliferating consumer society. Indeed, in view of the likely era of scarcity coming up we had better do so. But more of this below.

In short, my answer to those who find my scenario of a universal consumer standard gloomy is to point to the fact that the future will be gloomy willy-nilly, at least in the sense that our choices will be severely restricted. The growing consumer society will be an impossibility, except for a perhaps shrinking minority. The condition of a society which won't have to be held down by an irresponsible minority with a monopoly of force will be some such equalization as is adumbrated above. In a sense, the essential point I am putting forward is independent of the machinery of controls, allocations, and subsidies I referred to. It is that a society in which a substantial minority remains below the normal standard will be very unlikely to survive the steady state with its free institutions intact. A free society will have to have a universally available consumer standard, however this is realized. But I think it is clear that in the conditions of a technological society, it will have to be *realized*; it will not happen of itself. But once we accept this requirement of universality, we can see that with luck the prospect doesn't have to be all gloomy. Human happiness can survive the demise of the consumer society.

But we can't let optimism run away with us. A necessary condition of a steady state society with free institutions is probably some such universally available consumer standard. But this is far from being a sufficient condition. The dilemma we posed above remains intact. A universal standard society would represent a levelling down relative to our present society, and how can the affluent majority ever accept that? And if they can't, then how can this society be held together except by force? How does it admit any more of free institutions than the society whose inequalities are frozen in a permanent mould?

In a way to speak of a redistribution by levelling down is to put the prospect in a misleading way. If anyone proposed such a thing today there would be armed insurrection by the affluent and powerful. But we are talking about a quite different predicament with two stages. There is the transition, when dire shortages begin to appear, and then there is the new mould of a more permanent steady state society.

The transition may be a period of crisis, in which a kind of Dunkirk spirit may prevail, as in wartime, when people are willing to take a drop in the standard of living and even level down 'for the duration.' Whether this will happen, or an unseemly and brutal scramble for the scarce resources, is hard to predict or to determine. It depends on a number of intangibles in a people's public life.

But whether there can be a steady state society which doesn't slip towards authoritarian control is a question which arises after the transition granted this is weathered with free institutions unimpaired. And what will be required will be a sort of mutation in society's generally accepted self-definitions, the general sense of the nature of the social bond and the kind of solidarity which binds people. This is always a very mixed and varied thing, very difficult to describe or articulate. In our society today it is a mixture of national and/or ethnic/linguistic common identities on the one hand, and some notion of society as an interdependent enterprise of production for the general benefit on the other.

What kind of definition would sustain an equal universal-standard society pressed by the limits of the steady state? It would have to be a society with a very strong sense of common purpose. For only societies which feel a powerful common purpose or a forceful sense of common identity accept willingly the discipline of equal shares. Many societies, including our own, have a notion of a level of indigence below which no one should be allowed to fall. But this is very much an unequal portion, conferred in virtue of obligations of charity or universal justice. The sense, however, that things must be shared more or less equally comes from the sense that people share a common lot or face a common task. This is why this spirit is often visible in wartime. For many centuries the models that writers had in mind when thinking of such societies were the Greek *poleis*, but in our day the state of Israel might be usefully thought of as an example. Here there is both the forceful identity and the urgent common task.

Perhaps the health, maybe the fate, of free institutions in the steady state of the future depends on whether our societies respond to the end of growth either as a challenging common task which binds them or as a disaster in which each must scramble for safety on his own. One writer (Heilbroner) uses the image of a sinking liner in which everything depends on whether the passengers co-operate and file down in order, or rush in panic for the lifeboats which thus sink and take everyone to their doom. But in a way this image is partially misleading. For it makes us focus on the short-term crisis, which will be rather like that on the sinking liner. What is more important is the long haul. And for this another, more long-term, more deeply rooted sense of common purpose will be necessary. Men will have to respond to the end of growth not just as a crisis which requires that we all pull together; rather they will have to see in the new situation a new ideal form of life to be realized, and not just an occasion to show heroism in salvaging the old one. If we face the steady state as a set of challenging circumstances in which we are called on somehow to keep the flag aloft on endless production, we are probably lost. It is only if we come to see it as the occasion to realize a new kind of life in which the balance with nature is not a regrettable limit but an opportunity to express and realize new human possibilities that we shall be able to sustain the kind of public morale we will need to maintain the discipline of equality and hence free institutions.

In any case, a universal-standard society would have to be one with a strong sense of common purpose with the attendant sense of solidarity. Only in this context would the necessary degree of equality be seen as something acceptable. If we tried to make our present society more equal, there would be strong resistance from the affluent because they see such efforts as transfers in which they are forced to forgo income on behalf of essentially less productive people; and since they see the social bond largely as that of a co-operative enterprise of producers they don't see why they should support 'welfare bums.' But even in present society, affluent tax-payers don't have anything like so much resentment against what are perceived essentially as common enterprises. Even the much-maligned and cursed CBC is not resented in the same way as, say, laxer regulations on unemployment benefits.

But in another society with a stronger sense of common purpose, the allocations and subsidies which made the common standard universally available would be seen as common enterprises, essential to the goals of the society, rather than as transfers. Once they come to be seen in this latter light, the strains may become unbearable, as the resistance of the potentially affluent mounts. But seeing them this way is already to have lost some of the sense of common purpose; it is to see oneself as an individual bidding for scarce resources against rivals, rather than as the member of a common enterprise.

A universal-standard society would thus have to have this stronger purpose. And to this end, the advantage may lie with small societies or societies which can be meaningfully decentralized. For solidarity is difficult to maintain in very large societies, where relations are more and more mediated by bureaucratic structures and where masses of people feel an immense distance separating them from the decisions, achievements, and events which affect society as a whole.

And the advantage of smaller size is even more evident when we reflect on the conditions of maintaining free institutions. We saw that steady state societies will probably have to be much more planned and regulated than we are today. Their recurrent danger will be bureaucratic sclerosis, corruption, and exploitation by those in the know, accompanied by resignation, cynicism, and sporadic outbursts of violence on the part of the *administrés.* The only way to avoid this is to elaborate and keep alive mechanisms of consultation and popular decision in planning. How is the consensus on the universal consumer standard arrived at? How do we come to a common mind on this? Or is it in the end just handed down from an administrative structure which we each feel too powerless or perhaps too confused and uncertain to fight?

Perhaps the drive towards Byzantinism will be unbeatable. But if it can be beaten, this will much more probably occur in small societies or societies which can be meaningfully decentralized – that is where the units of decentralization are not just arbitrarily carved out (as are most urban electoral constituencies or the boundaries of a development zone for example), but have a meaning in the common and differential sense of identity of those who live within them. The elaboration of a consensus, the discussion of alternatives, the referring back to citizens, are all potentially feasible in small units in a way that has no parallel in larger ones.

It is often said that we need to elaborate new techniques of consultation/decision, and that we need to apply our considerable communications technology, film, television, and so on, to this end. Some of the successes of social animation have shown the truth in this. But these are successes in small societies. In large societies this same communication technology can be as much a barrier as a link. When a mass of citizens feel an unbridgeable distance between them and the source and process of decision, television doesn't bridge the gap. Rather it becomes just another way of moulding the image of that process of decision as something essentially foreign and unknown directly to them.

Another condition of continued solidarity in a steady state society will probably be mobility, the ability to change profession during a lifetime or between generations. Turn-over of this kind is an important condition of a sense of equality, and this is essential to the sense of solidarity in societies which have evolved beyond class-differentiation.

Let us try to gather together the threads by returning to the central question, somewhat rephrased: as we enter the steady state society, is there any way of avoiding the strong trend towards an authoritarian and Byzantine society, towards the atrophy if not destruction of civil rights and the institutions of self-government, and the growth of an all-embracing irresponsible bureaucratic control of our lives?

I started to answer this question by asking how a steady state society could meet the demand for equality which seemed a condition of the continued unity without which self-governing institutions don't survive. The answer seemed to be a society with a universally available consumption standard. And a condition of this in turn would seem to be a society with a powerful sense of common purpose. In order to remain vitally self-governing in a steady state, a society will have to elaborate new ways of popular consultation and decision. And it should in addition be highly mobile. For all these reasons it had better be small or capable of meaningful decentralization.

But we could also run through our thumbnail portrait of the alternative society from this angle. Plainly, steady state societies will have to be planned and regulated as ours are not. There is not just the question of allocation of scarce resources discussed above; but the whole direction of technological development will have to be consciously guided towards a recycling technology, which will rely more heavily on abundant resources and forms of energy and production which respect certain pollution limits. A society like this can only avoid sclerosis and Byzantinism if it can compensate with a more vigorous participation by citizens in consultation and decisions. A society which is small and can decentralize will have a great advantage in this.

But a society in this predicament can only combat Byzantinism by keeping open as well the opportunities for individual or small group initiative. And this, too, requires decentralization. It should be possible for people to elaborate new and original ways of living in balance with nature with a low use of energy and resources. The need for leeway to allow for different ways of realizing a steady state should eventually force us to reverse the trend towards the concentration of population in a few large urban centres. But the partial return to a larger number of smaller, more self-sufficient communities will probably be a technical imperative of the steady state in any case.

But what must go on binding society together, however decentralized into diverse communities, is the strong sense of being engaged in a common enterprise; for without this, diversification will soon mean striking inequality in access to essential common resources, and with this a free, self-governing society is in jeopardy.

It may indeed be very difficult to combine both decentralization and a strong sense of purpose, and this double requirement may push this sketch of an alternative future even farther towards the utopian fringe. But both these conditions seem essential to a free and participating society in the new predicament arising beyond the end of growth.

I'd now like to take up the question which has been the implicit focus of this discussion: what are our chances in this country of making the transition to a steady state without sliding into authoritarian or bureaucratic rule?

Well, we clearly have some advantages. First we are a small society relatively speaking. But more important, since 22 millions is still a lot of people, we are a society which admits of meaningful decentralization. Indeed, this fact - that the constituent parts of Canada have a meaningful identity - has been our major political problem since the beginning and may indeed break the country up.

But it may turn out in the coming age to be a tremendous advantage. We only have to think of how difficult it will be in larger, more centralized nations to plan for the steady state without entrenching and extending a bureaucratic structure so distant and irresponsible that the vast majority will experience it only as an alien force. Decentralization in England, France, even the United States may be of no avail because the units will not have the identity which they need to function as units, where citizens sense enough of a common identity as members of that unit to want to participate in shaping its course.

But the division of Canada into provinces represents in most cases an important sociological reality. In some cases provinces, in others, groups of provinces, embody a distinct society, with a culture and history and in one case a language distinct from those dominant elsewhere. It is realistic to see these as units of autonomous planning - indeed, it would be very unrealistic to see our future any other way; Canada is an uncentralizable country. This is a fact that many reformers used to curse; they are now beginning to be grateful for it. For the chances of controlling a distant and irresponsible bureaucracy, although perhaps not great anywhere in the coming age, are infinitely greater in these smaller societies.

Planning in Canada for the steady state will obviously have to be greatly decentralized. For instance, the elaboration of the standard pattern of consumption could vary somewhat from region to region. Ultimately, it would be a healthy thing if our regions evolved away from the homogenization of their ways of life which has been steadily going ahead in past decades.

Decentralization we can have for the asking. But can we combine this with a common purpose? This has been our recurrent problem and it will return with a vengeance in the era of the steady state. And as ever one of the crucial determinants of the outcome will be the question of equality. For some of our most persistent and divisive inequalities have been interregional. A century of growth has not appreciably reduced them for reasons with which we are increasingly familiar and which were mentioned above. Left to itself exponential growth increases gaps, as we see on the international scene. The effect of interregional transfers by governments and migration in the last decades has probably been to offset this tendency so that the inequalities remain roughly the same. But here, as elsewhere, growth is now considered the palliative. Even if they cannot attain equality, poorer regions may feel an incentive to remain on board in order to participate in the growth of the larger Canadian economy. I believe that this incentive is the major counter-force to independentism in Quebec; indeed it may be the decisive factor preventing a majority of Québecois from opting out.

The coming era of scarcity will generate its own incentives for us to stick together: the need to pool resource endowments, the need to make a common front against an external world which will more and more press us to give up our resources quickly and cheaply. All this provides an important potential basis for co-operation and indeed makes it essential. But in politics the essential is not always the actual, and we will probably need to do much better in reducing inter-regional inequality if we are to generate the common purpose to realize this potential.

But the transition to the steady state will give us an unprecedented chance to do better. Of itself, the new predicament may change the balance of economic importance of different occupations and hence regions. For instance, food production is almost certainly going to command a greater relative reward in the new dispensation.

But beyond this, the transition will involve a far-reaching transformation of our economy, as we have seen. We will have to shift our effort to quite different technologies, those of recycling, low resource use, and the offsetting of pollution effects. This by itself means the building up of whole new industries, a development of the same type as but on a larger scale than the growth of the computer and information-processing industry in the last decades. And in addition, the existing industries will have to transform their production pattern in important ways to meet the new requirements of resource utilization and pollution control. And all this will have to be done under public direction in a way that earlier transformations were not.

Will we be able to use this opportunity to disperse the new technologies and industries more evenly, so that all regions have some comparable part in their development? In a way, this is a much more hopeful prospect than that of dispersing an already developed industry by moving an extra branch plant out to a neglected area; for this kind of development runs against an existing grain and is usually accomplished by lavish public bribes which turn out to be bad investments.

In the end the crucial question may be whether the will is there in the rich heartland of the country to back such a policy of dispersal. And whether this is so will depend on a number of things both intangible and unpredictable.

In a way this sums up our situation. We are in a rare, almost unique position to enter the new age beyond growth. We have not only the advantage of decentralization, but also the very substantial ones of great resource endowment, so that in many cases we can afford to ease ourselves into the new dispensation instead of being brutally hurled into it; of wide open spaces which make at least some of our pollution limits less immediately pressing than those of other countries; of great wealth per head in capital and technical know-how, so that we could ourselves design and effect many of the new industries and technologies which we require. We are in a relatively favoured international position.

Apart from the too great economic leverage which the United States has over us (admittedly a not inconsiderable factor) our principal obstacle to reacting in a timely and creative way to the coming crisis is an internal one. Canadians are still deeply wedded to the consumer society, and at the same time very uncertain of their own powers to pioneer a new economic mode of life. The consumer society itself is seen as largely an American creation from which we have benefitted by our integration into the American economy.

This integration tends to paralyse our will all the more in that it is piecemeal. Provincial governments agree to sell off various natural resources to multinational corporations, often on bad terms even for themselves, all too frequently on terms which further reduce our future freedom to respond intelligently as a society to the coming era of scarcity. When this mood is on them, provincial governments and electorates want to block any common initiatives towards a new conserving policy, and they do this in the name of development, through which they see their only conceivably economic salvation.

And this could be our fate. We could be incapable of creating a new structure to meet the new predicament, because we lack the will and above all the common will to do so. We could be hamstrung by what is potentially our greatest strength, our regional diversity. So that as pressures mount we could be thrown into a scramble for survival, in which some regions respond to the world's growing hunger for resources by selling them fast at astronomical prices, perhaps investing the proceeds in traditional technologies which won't be sustainable when the resources are gone (what good is a petrochemical plant if we burn all our oil for fuel?), while others cope with mounting scarcity by costly imports. The image of the sinking liner comes again irresistibly to mind.

Perhaps any sober prophet of the future would have to pick this gloomy prospect as the most likely one. But the compulsive optimist in me sees signs of another trend. There also are in Canada: a mounting concern about our economic integration into the United States; a very ill-defined but potentially powerful feeling about the land, particularly the North, and a sense that it is ecologically threatened; a growing resistance to resource management (or mismanagement) by the multinationals, and a sense that it is not in our interest; a growing desire not to go the same way as the United States towards the ultimate of bigness and mobility, and the sacrifice of the past to the future. Some of these trends I may have imagined, and some I have exaggerated, but something like them is there.

The question is whether these diverse sentiments and aspirations – some of them hard-headed perceptions of interest, others which feed on our sense of identity and the way this is sustained by the past and what surrounds us (aspirations which can all too easily run into conflict) – can be brought together into a common objective, united in the project of an alternative society. This is by no means inevitable, but I do not believe it is impossible. But it will take a number of things, including two which are equally hard to produce to order: good luck and creative political leadership.

In the meantime, while the issue of the future society beyond growth still cannot be posed at the centre of our political life, we can nevertheless make partial gains. Any setback to the heedless and reckless development of our natural resources for export, any successful measure to safeguard the environment, any shift in our priorities towards the universal provision of a decent normal standard of life, puts us in a marginally better posture to face the coming transition. Perhaps the big difference, whether we respond creatively as a free society, will be determined by a number of small decisions, some of which we can make today.

The land of participation

CLAUDE CASTONGUAY

Social progress in the world of tomorrow

Whenever we speculate about the future of man, we cannot avoid taking his past record into account. And it is hard to deny that the closer one looks at this record, the more uneven and limited human progress appears. Indeed, history seems to consist of an endless series of struggles between nations, of which the Second World War, by virtue of the intensity with which it was waged and the untold devastation left in its wake, may be regarded as the culmination. Yet despite the suffering caused by that war, and the countless local conflicts which have gone on more or less uninterruptedly since it ended, mankind continues to accumulate increasingly powerful weapons of destruction, to the point that, in the event of a third world war, it would be possible to eradicate every form of life from the earth.

At the same time, there has been a spectacular increase in knowledge, particularly in the exact sciences, such as mathematics, physics, chemistry, and electronics. It should be stressed, however, that the constant search for higher standards of material comfort and better weapons has been to a large extent responsible for this technological progress.

The social sciences, on the other hand, lacking this spur to constant improvement, have evolved much more slowly. It is only recently that those whose professional interest lies in the way human societies function and relate to one another – the economists, sociologists, and political scientists – have reached the point where they can help us understand the past and the present; it is rather premature to expect them to predict the future with any degree of accuracy. Similarly, in the behavioural sciences even the most expert psychologists have a great deal of ground to make up before they can speak with the same authority as their colleagues in biology.

It is only within the last two centuries that a sizable proportion of the human race has enjoyed the benefits of the material progress to which I have just referred. Despite all the impressive advances in production methods, in the provision of new services, and the efficient use of natural resources, however, more than half of the people on this planet live in conditions which may be properly described as inhuman.

Yet throughout the course of its slow and painful evolution, mankind has demonstrated astonishing reserves of patience and optimism. It is these qualities which, handed down from one generation to the next, lie behind the daily toil of countless men and women, as well as their ability to transcend their condition in every possible sphere. In most cases, it requires very little motivation to tap these reserves, given mankind's unquenchable desire for knowledge and self-improvement. Human fallibility and, at the same time, this instinctive love of progress, however great the obstacles, should be borne in mind as we reflect for a few moments on some of the ways in which society may evolve.

THE CLUB OF ROME

To provide a framework for these reflections, I have elected to relate them specifically to the first report of the Club of Rome, a document which, using methods that themselves bear witness to human ingenuity, gives a clear picture of what the future of the human race might be.

According to this report, the behaviour model of the global system may be described in terms of an exponential growth of population and capital, followed by the collapse of the system. In other words, the fact that world population, consumption of all kinds, and pollution are increasing at an ever-accelerating rate can only result in the depletion of resources essential to human life. Such a view, of course, presupposes the continuance of current trends. To support their hypothesis – a highly questionable one, to my mind – the authors of the report introduce multiple variables into their equations, concluding that mere technological changes, of whatever nature or scope, will in no way alter the basic characteristics of the current global system; technological innovations, at best, would merely delay the collapse of the system as predicted, since they do not affect the inexorable drift towards infinity which is inherent in any exponential growth system.

There seems little point at the moment in looking beyond the general conclusion of this report and its far-reaching implications as neither of the premises on which its conclusions are based appears to me to stand up to close analysis.

In essence, the Club of Rome report defines the problem as one of exponential growth, that is to say unlimited growth, of population, consumption, and pollution, in a world where there is a limited supply of resources. Wherever consumption, for example, follows an exponential curve, available resources, however plentiful, are bound to be depleted sooner or later.

The human capacity for predicting the future, as anyone who has ever tried it will agree, is strictly limited. And where the prediction concerns the future of the world as a whole, over a relatively extended period of time, the range of possibilities becomes so vast that the prophet has little but his imagination to guide him. To take but one example in the field of demography, the unexpected evolution in the birth rate in recent decades, together with our limited knowledge of the underlying causes of this evolution, illustrate that it is currently impossible to make projections in this area with any degree of accuracy for periods longer than thirty years.

Moreover, we have no accurate figures concerning current rates of consumption of natural, non-renewable resources; new sources of energy unthought of twenty-five years ago are in the process of being harnessed; the oceans of the world are beginning to yield some of their vast potential as a new source of food; rapid changes are taking place in people's needs, and in the way they use available resources. In other words, there are simply too many variables for us to measure with any hope of accuracy the resources which mankind currently has at its disposal. Moreover, we have witnessed too many inaccurate forecasts in recent years, particularly in the field of technology, to place complete trust in the projections contained in the Club of Rome report – even though they were arrived at with the help of computer programs.

It should also be stressed that these global predictions, together with the momentous inferences which can be drawn from them, are not especially pertinent to the Canadian situation. In Canada, population density and growth are equally low in relation to the size of the country, while supplies of natural resources and potential agricultural yield are more than adequate for the needs of the people, even using current methods of exploitation.

These two factors – low population density and abundant resources – compel us in Canada to look beyond the generalities of the Club of Rome's findings. It would be totally unrealistic, in my view, to curb the rate of economic and demographic growth in Canada on the grounds that the global system is said to be about to collapse, since there is no evidence that such a disaster is about to take place in the immediate future. Besides, could Canada morally accept a reduction in our help to the less fortunate nations of the earth, where millions of people are presently engaged in a daily struggle against poverty and hunger, simply because of the possibility of this hypothetical disaster?

Summing up, I believe that the real merit of the Club of Rome report lies in reminding us that we cannot afford, either socially or economically, to allow the global system to continue growing indefinitely at its current pace. The authors, like a number of other observers before them, rightly underline the urgent need to manage growth, to put an end to the conspicuous squandering of non-renewable resources, and to protect our natural environment.

THE FAILINGS OF THE CONSUMER SOCIETY

Increasing attention is being paid among the developed nations to the issues raised by the Club of Rome report. But there are other areas of concern, just as serious and no less deserving of our consideration, to which I should now like to turn.

One of the chief consequences of the Industrial Revolution was to put economic growth in the forefront of national priorities. This was only to be expected, as millions of men and women, for the first time in the history of the human race, had the opportunity of enjoying some degree of material comfort, thus freeing themselves from the meaningless drudgery which had hitherto characterized their lives. However, the sustained pursuit of this particular goal over the last two centuries has resulted in the situation with which we are all familiar, whereby for an increasing number of the inhabitants of the so-called developed nations human life has become subservient to the overriding imperative of growth. The suffering caused by the depression of the 1930s and by the ensuing world war merely strengthened the widespread belief in the principle of sustained growth. It is only in recent years that we have gradually become aware of the shortcomings of a society in which the very lives of the citizens, their aspirations as well as their decisions, are to a large extent subordinated to the growth syndrome.

Thus the concept and the nature of work have been distorted. At present we value only those activities which are profitable, while despising many time-honoured tasks on the sole grounds that they do not contribute to an increase in production. Work, defined simply as one factor contributing to productivity rather than as a natural human activity, has become increasingly degraded and brutalized.

Uninterrupted growth has also led to the creation of vast corporate empires of ever-increasing size and complexity, upsetting the delicate balance of power between producers, labour, and consumers. Moreover, the rapid expansion of advertising and of credit facilities as additional stimuli to consumers has helped create a situation in which most workers find themselves locked into a frantic cycle of work and consumption, while others, who do not have access to remunerative employment, are simply excluded from the system. Further consequences of this growth-consumption cycle include the tendency for many large corporations to make excessive profits, for some persons to get much richer while the relative or absolute impoverishment of others increases.

Moreover, in a society in which economic growth dominates other national priorities, it is virtually inevitable that programs or measures designed to redistribute wealth are doomed to at least partial failure. In the Canadian context, for example, more energetic government measures in this direction would inevitably result in reduced profits for Canadian firms, thereby making them less competitive in world markets. Even so, it remains intolerable to find large numbers of people still living in conditions of genuine poverty in an affluent society where our natural resources and productive capacity are sufficient to ensure everyone a high standard of living.

This commitment to economic growth for its own sake has other far-reaching effects. It fosters a brand of consumerism in which the creativity, the aptitude for work, the independent judgment, and the active participation in community affairs of individual citizens tend to be eroded. Too much affluence leads inevitably, it would seem, to a disavowal of effort and involvement. Clearly, there is something drastically wrong with the value system of a society which places such a high premium on the accumulation of consumer goods. It is hardly surprising, in such a society, to discover a dramatic decline in standards of individual behaviour and responsibility, together with an increase of violence in various forms. In particular, there is the violence of the written and spoken word, which, spreading quickly through society with the help of modern communications, breeds intolerance between all those, whether individuals or groups, who do not happen to share the same point of view; between people of different races or ethnic backgrounds, between unions and employers, and between different ideologies.

Another equally striking consequence of our system of priorities is the decay of our urban and rural environment. As the city centres are taken over for the exclusive use of business and commercial activities, immediately adjoining areas begin to deteriorate. Suburbs, which lack the amenities essential for a well-balanced community life, proliferate. The construction of expressways and ever larger downtown parking facilities leads to a serious displacement of residential areas and thus to increased commuting distances. Rural communities are debilitated by the departure of their more dynamic inhabitants. These are some of the more visible signs of our deteriorating environment, resulting more or less directly from decisions taken with short-term, economic objectives in mind rather than the needs of human habitation.

The social costs of this deterioration – in increased crime, drug-abuse, individual maladjustment, and chronic unemployment – are becoming all too obvious to anyone with the slightest interest in his immediate society. And the ecological costs, in pollution of all kinds, are just as staggering.

Clearly, then, our consumer society has reached the point where a thoroughgoing revision of our priorities and scale of values is urgently required. Particularly in a country like Canada, where both production and consumption comfortably exceed our basic requirements, it is imperative that we adopt a more truly humane approach to development, whereby the role of work, the distribution of wealth, housing, social services, and the safeguarding of the environment are defined according to the real needs of people, and are no longer mere byproducts of policies adopted with primarily economic aims in mind.

In recommending the adoption of such a philosophy, I am not suggesting that we halt economic growth entirely, but rather that we learn to regard it as a means to an end and not as an end in itself. We need growth as a stimulus to our economy, if only to provide the increased resources wherever they are lacking, both at home and abroad. In future, however, our combined efforts ought to be directed to regulating growth - namely to check the wasteful use of resources and the pollution of the environment. Nor do I wish to imply for a moment that we should dismantle the present social system completely and start all over again. Even if this were possible, industrial society has brought too many tangible benefits to mankind for us to entertain such a radical solution. Still, even the path of reform, such as I have in mind, involves a considerable disruption of an existing frame of mind and style of life. It is bound to meet with stiff opposition; certain financial interests, in particular, are likely to fight to the last to preserve the power which they currently wield in our society.

To face up to such a challenge involves a belief that man is as interested in shaping the fate of his environment as he is in technological innovation and that he can conceive of progress in other than simply materialistic terms.

NEW VALUES, NEW OBJECTIVES

As I have indicated, a society which sets in the forefront the full development of its citizens must have a new scale of priorities which takes precedence over the aims and decisions of the economic sphere. The chief problem is not so much one of defining these material, social, and cultural needs as of discovering how to introduce the necessary changes into the social system without completely disrupting it. In addition, it will be no small task to convince people not only that such changes are possible, but that they will enhance the quality of life. In fact, what is really needed, before we can build a new society, is a radical change in our outlook.

There have been many attempts to classify human needs, some authorities dividing them into different types, others relating them to specific social groups. The importance of these studies lies not so much in their completeness (or otherwise) as in what they tell us about certain principles of behaviour, certain basic human characteristics which tend to produce the various needs and which have to be taken into account if those needs are to be satisfied. When it comes to determining the new priorities referred to above, three principles of crucial importance will need to be borne in mind.

1 In the first place, I am firmly convinced that society should not be directly responsible for the development of individual citizens; rather, it ought to provide them with the proper conditions and the necessary means to achieve self-fulfilment by their own efforts. This principle is based on the deep-rooted human need for independence and recognizes that the individual should be free to make the major decisions regarding his personal and social life, in so far as this is possible.

2 The second basic principle which should be observed is that of distributive justice, or, to use a more familiar expression, equality of opportunity. It implies that every member of society should enjoy a fair share of the material comforts and the services which it provides, in order to be able to realize his or her potential as an individual and as a citizen.

3 The third basic requirement, in my view, is a system whereby the individual can participate in the process of defining objectives and reaching decisions affecting the community to which he belongs, by virtue of his daily toil, as well as culturally and politically. The success of such a system depends, in turn, on his being adequately informed about the issues concerned.

Man, as I see him (and her), is responsible for his own development, while simultaneously contributing to the improvement of the community as a whole. In return for his labour, by virtue of the principle of equality of opportunity, the community should provide him with sufficient goods and services to allow him to grow as an individual, and should also allow him, through political structures designed and organized for that purpose, to participate in shaping the aims and decisions of his community.

Turning now to our analysis of human needs, I should like to consider them under four headings: (1) basic needs, related to survival; (2) those which allow the individual to function; (3) those related to his development, both as an individual and as a member of society; (4) the need for man to use, in a rational manner, the limited resources at his disposal, and to preserve his natural environment.

1 / Basic needs
Obviously, these include the provision of food, clothing, and adequate shelter. In a prosperous society such as ours, where the individual citizen enjoys a considerable degree of personal freedom, these needs are normally met by the provision of income, enabling him not merely to survive but to maintain himself and his dependants at what society considers a normal level. This income may take one

of two possible forms: either wages paid in return for work, or payments resulting from measures designed to redistribute income (a topic to which we shall return). Among basic needs we should also include adequate housing, that is to say housing which not only meets accepted standards of sanitation, but provides the space and the comfort which every individual requires to lead a normal healthy existence. Finally, adequate schooling and job-training, to enable him to turn his abilities to advantage, should also be placed in this first category.

2/Needs relating to the functioning of the individual within society
Among this category of supportive services, in addition to the schools and jobs already mentioned, adequate health, social services, legal and transport facilities (for the conduct of daily business) may be regarded as a bare minimum, if the individual is to function properly as a member of society. And while it is impossible, within the limits of the present paper, to examine in detail the question of the extent of these services, how many are needed and of what quality, and how they should be organized, there is one point concerning their availability which must be stressed: every member of the public should have access to them (geographically as well as financially speaking) and the relevant information should be disseminated as widely as possible. Moreover, they should be organized in such a way as to remove any barriers (psychological or otherwise) that might discourage people from using them, and with sufficient flexibility to permit the concentration of available resources in those areas where there is a particular need for them, as in the case of the disabled.

3/Needs related to individual development
Clearly, we cannot hope to give an accurate description of this category of needs, which vary according to the tastes, abilities, age, and background of the individual concerned. On the other hand, some at least may be identified, since they are consistent with what appear to be fairly widespread human aspirations. First and foremost, in this connection, is the need for an environment conducive to the creation and preservation of a stable family milieu, of vital importance in the rearing of normal healthy children. The existence of such an environment depends on a multiplicity of factors, ranging from good quality housing to the rational utilization of space (especially urban space) and the development of a sense of belonging to the community.

In the same category, we should have to include those needs relating to creativity, development of the personality, cultural stimuli of all kinds, and the use of leisure. The importance of this area of human needs is widely recognized nowadays, so there is little point in my emphasizing it, except perhaps to recall in passing that while considerable lip-service is paid in our affluent society to man's creative and cultural activities, the proportion of the national budget currently devoted to encouraging them is minute, as compared to the sums spent on the production of material goods – with all the waste of resources and attendant pollution that such a policy implies.

Before leaving this category, let me repeat that the possibility for the individual of participating in decisions affecting the life of the community is a basic requirement of a truly humane society. Given the importance which I attach to this principle, I shall return to it later.

4 / The need to use resources rationally

If the wastage and pollution referred to at the beginning of this paper are to be checked, it is clear that mankind will have to modify both current methods of production and the rates of consumption directly linked to them. But this is a vast and complex issue which, unfortunately, cannot be gone into here.

These categories of human needs, of course, are only approximations, a fact that in itself is a reminder that we still have a great deal more to learn about certain aspects of human behaviour. How does each individual acquire the set of values which governs his behaviour? Is education the determining factor in acquiring these values? What are the ground rules which enable us to live in harmony with our neighbours? Why is it that groups of different ethnic or racial background are able to coexist amicably in some countries but not in others? Questions such as these underline the fact that a much more thorough understanding of social behaviour is required before we can identify and eventually satisfy mankind's real needs.

WORK

At the moment, man's needs are satisfied for the most part, in three ways: by the payment of wages in exchange for work; by income security plans; and by the various supportive services to which I have already alluded. I should like to look at the first two of these methods in somewhat greater detail.

In Canada, a variety of policies and programs have been adopted with a view to stimulating and regulating economic growth. One of the primary objectives of these measures has been to fight unemployment by creating jobs in sufficient quantity to meet current demand. We also have a large number of job-training and retraining schemes designed to help workers to adapt themselves to periodic fluctuations in the economy or the labour market. At the same time, the government has introduced a number of income security plans, whose function is, first, to bear some of the individual's financial responsibilities for his family, and second, to provide support for the individual in the event of his being unemployed.

They also provide a minimum income for those who, for one reason or another, are unable to work. Programs such as these, backed up by an abundance of natural resources and an industrious population, account for the high standard of living currently enjoyed by most Canadians, one that is undoubtedly the envy of many other nations.

While the over-all situation may be described as healthy, there are many disparities and discrepancies between individuals and between one part of the country and the next. And, over and above these readily discernible problems, there is another which, although harder to pinpoint, must be regarded as extremely serious, since it represents a challenge to the very notion of work, and the way work is organized in our society.

Signs of a deep-seated malaise in the attitude people take with regard to work are becoming increasingly widespread. They include rising absenteeism, poor quality workmanship, labour disputes which break out without warning, jobs which lie vacant despite the availability of qualified (and unemployed) workers to fill them, and so on. Many people are convinced that it is the welfare system, which, by allowing people to lead a comfortable existence without working, is largely responsible for the growth of these social evils. Personally, I find this view untenable. In the first place, in a consumer society such as ours, the vast majority of people are only too anxious to hold down a well-paid job. Moreover, it is simply not true that welfare payments enable people to live comfortably; the large number of individuals and families currently living in conditions of poverty make this abundantly clear. (The fact that some workers periodically withdraw from the labour market as soon as they have worked long enough to qualify for unemployment benefits tends to obscure this aspect of the problem.) The roots of the problem are much deeper.

To begin with, there is a clear connection between these negative attitudes towards work and the fact that the nature of work itself has been gradually transformed over the years, to the point that, for an ever-growing segment of the population, it has lost whatever meaning it once had. When work is defined in strictly utilitarian terms, as merely one component in the production process, the individual worker has to adapt himself to whatever changes in schedules, machinery, or output that that process may require. In addition, both employers and unions (although for very different reasons) have seen fit to encourage specialization to such an extent that the worker, finding it impossible to identify himself with the product he has helped to create, tends to become apathetic. Perceiving himself as a mere cog in the production/consumption cycle, living under the constant threat of unemployment due to the closing-down or reorganization of factories, he feels increasing frustration and alienation; the rising incidence of nervous breakdowns, alcoholism, absenteeism, together with the frequently deplored deterioration in standards of workmanship are the more visible signs of such feelings. The indifference shown by many workers during work-stoppages towards the smooth running or indeed the very survival of the firm that employs them may be regarded as equally symptomatic.

In other words, man seems well on the way to rejecting a concept of work defined primarily in terms of its contribution to economic growth. Workers appear increasingly drawn to jobs which will give them a chance to use their natural creativity and thus achieve some measure of personal satisfaction and self-fulfilment, jobs, moreover, which are considered significant by the society in which they live. In fact, a new concept of work - as opposed to drudgery - appears to be evolving, whereby technological and economic forces are being enlisted in the service of mankind rather than the other way round.

Given the fact that work is crucial to man's existence, as much for his self-realization as for his material survival, I am convinced that this new concept, which appears to be developing within (and despite) the present economic system, gives a clear indication of the direction in which society ought to be moving. Consequently, I should like to look at some of the ways of bringing about the changes that will be required if work is indeed to take on a new meaning and become more satisfying for the individual and more creative for society as a whole. I shall begin by looking at changes relating to the structure and organization of work, and then consider the impact such changes would have with respect to the income security system.

As a first objective, every worker, no matter the type of enterprise he works for, should feel genuinely involved in its activities and not feel like a mere cog in a machine. There are various ways in which this can be achieved. Co-operative systems offer a number of advantages and certainly deserve to be introduced on a much wider scale. Stock and profit-sharing schemes can also be extremely effective; tax concessions and increased credit facilities might be used to encourage their growth. In every type of organization, public or private, efforts will have to be made to designate the specific areas in which workers might most usefully participate in the decision-making process. It should be emphasized, however, that participation only achieves the desired results in so far as it is genuine: it should not be thought of as a gimmick, a kind of safety-valve brought in from time to time to reduce tension between workers and employers. In those cases where it has been tried and found wanting, it was usually not the principle itself that was at fault, so much as the fact that the status of the workers concerned remained exactly as it was before the experiment was undertaken. These so-called failures certainly do not constitute grounds for obstructing progress along what is no doubt the only road likely to lead to improved labour relations, namely a whole-hearted involvement on the part of the worker in the affairs of the company that employs him.

Another task will be the elimination of the welter of obstacles which currently inhibit entry into the labour market. In too many cases, these restrictions, which were introduced by professional organizations, unions, and government with the ostensible aim of protecting workers and the general public alike, defeat their own ends by their unwarranted severity and become merely self-serving in the interests of the highest paid employees.

Every possible effort should be made to improve the status of the many types of work which, although not necessarily profitable in commercial terms, nevertheless have a worthwhile contribution to make to individual and community life. At the moment, too many jobs lie vacant, while others are not created simply because economic considerations and an inflexible labour market tend to obscure their real value. In such areas as health and education, job-training and rehabilitation, and the use of leisure, there is room for considerably expanded services and thus a variety of new jobs.

If workers in all spheres are to be given a chance to increase their knowledge and skills, a much wider range of educational facilities will be required, including refresher courses, sabbatical years, ongoing programs for adults, and so on. The possibility of obtaining better working conditions or, alternatively, more time off for personal or community activities in exchange for lower income should also be explored.

The fact that one can discover, within every community, a host of needs that our existing organizations – no doubt because of their too rigid structure – are ill-equipped to satisfy, is not only something to be deplored: it also represents a tremendous challenge, all the more so in that it will be up to those most directly affected, each according to his special talents, and with the help of more flexible work patterns, to determine the areas in which improvements are most needed. The financing of such projects will raise particular problems, since those responsible for them will have to ensure that public funds are not being squandered without, however, having recourse to the rigid controls or a cut-and-dried division of work that would be against the whole spirit of what they are trying to achieve. On the other hand, these difficulties will be alleviated inasmuch as the allocation of more funds to community projects is likely to ease the strain on social security.

From this brief outline, it will be apparent that there are many obstacles that will have to be overcome before the notion, that work should be as meaningful for the individual as it is socially beneficial, becomes a reality. However, the long-term effectiveness of these proposals will depend on the extent to which the individual can choose the area in which he or she wishes to be active, through the existence of appropriate income security measures. Without these measures such freedom of choice could not exist. If work is to be at once creative and productive, the worker will have to be freed of the constraints currently imposed by a highly organized, rigidly structured labour market.

Efforts to bring about the changes I have been discussing – even though these changes are based on real, identifiable human needs – are bound to meet with all kinds of opposition, the nature and extent of which can only be touched upon briefly in this paper.

A major source of resistance to change is the traditional notion of work held by those who are currently in positions of authority or have already lived a major part of their adult life. What will be required of this influential section of the population is nothing less than a complete rethinking of a value system that they (and society as a whole) have come to regard as the very basis of progress and social stability. To make matters worse, we are proposing to replace their traditional view by a concept which, in their eyes, cannot fail to encourage laziness, erosion of authority and property rights, and a never-ending cycle of claims.

The apathy shown by far too many workers, together with the belligerency of certain union leaders, as a result of which many employers keep their contacts with union representatives to the absolute minimum, are not likely to make progress any easier. Sweeping changes will be required within the unions and in professional organizations generally; leaders and rank and file alike will have to show much more concern than they have in the past for the smooth operation of the enterprises that employ them, while at the same time paying more attention to the significance that work has acquired in the lives of their members. The search for new objectives and a new philosophy of work will in itself give unions and professional corporations a new sense of purpose; perhaps they will be drawn together in the common effort to explore and to improve conditions of everyday life in society at large.

Of the many related problems that will have to be solved if the status of work is really to be changed, two in particular deserve mention, however briefly. The present income security programs will have to be modified in such a way that the individual worker has a wider choice among the different kinds of work and employment available; and we shall need more flexible methods of financing community projects, the viability of which ought not to be determined only by such narrow criteria as profitability and administrative efficiency.

Summing up, one can say that the hardest part of all this will be to change the ingrained mental attitudes of a large segment of the population. Finally – and more optimistically – let us not forget that what we usually refer to, for want of a better term, as the labour pool will be expanding much more slowly in the future, due to the falling birth rate; this factor should alleviate to some extent the difficulties I have listed.

THE SECURITY OF INCOME

Although Canadian income security programs compare favourably with those of other industrial countries, they are still far from perfect, in that they are only partially successful in effecting a fair redistribution of national wealth. Thus in 1972 – the latest year for which detailed information on family incomes is now available from Statistics Canada – the average income for the five million families then living in Canada was $11,300, with a distribution spread that ranged from the 345,000 families whose income was less than $3,000 to the 190,000 with annual incomes of more than $25,000. In that year, 20 per cent of Canadian families had incomes of less than $5,516, i.e. 49 per cent of the family income just mentioned for the country as a whole. Putting it another way, no less than a million Canadian families managed to exist on annual incomes of less than half the national average. What makes these figures even more striking is the fact that these same lower-income families (a fifth of the nation) earned between them only 6 per cent of the total national income. At the other end of the scale, the top 20 per cent of families in the upper-income brackets managed to earn 39 per cent of that total.

When comparing statistics covering recent decades, it is clear that despite the increases in social security benefits and the existence of a progressive income tax system, the distribution of income among Canadians has remained substantially the same over the last twenty years. The share of the total family income received by the bottom fifth of the population has not risen, while that of the 20 per cent with high incomes has not decreased. One should not, however, conclude from these figures that the present social security system is entirely ineffective. Without it, for example, in 1972, the same bottom fifth of the population would have received only 3.5 per cent of the national total, rather than 6 per cent.

Figures such as these make it abundantly clear that if we are to eliminate poverty and allow those workers who are at present locked into frustrating jobs – jobs they only took in the first place in order to boost inadequate family incomes and which they find themselves unable to leave because of the rigid structure of the labour market – to have the chance of seeking more remunerative and satisfying employment, the redistributive feature of the income security system will have to be greatly improved.

Progress in this direction will require the abolition of income tax for all persons whose income falls below a certain agreed level of basic support, while at the same time eliminating the administrative categories into which various recipients of aid are presently divided. In the interests of fairness and the preservation of individual freedom, financial support with respect to housing or child care will have to be made directly available through the income security programs themselves, rather than by subsidizing these services. Such an approach has the additional advantage of avoiding the excessive taxation of income increases which result when tax devices are designed to recover part of these payments.

Finally, the evolution of redistribution measures will entail the replacement of social assistance by a genuine guaranteed minimum income program which, either through negative income tax, or tax credits, would provide support both to those outside the labour market and to those whose incomes fall below pre-determined levels. One of the principal effects of the new program would be to remove the barriers preventing access to the labour market (and which the present system helped set up), thus fostering the workers' need to be productive, while making a contribution to society. Indeed, in a society in which the status of individual and community work is enhanced, where the worker has more freedom of choice with respect to the kind of work he wants to do, and where, as a consequence, the whole concept of a 'labour market' has a different meaning, the income needs of the citizens could not be defined and met without the implementation of the guaranteed annual income.

Obviously, this concept needs to be examined much more closely before it can be introduced; but, as a basic principle, it indicates the direction in which Canada should be moving, if all its citizens are to be engaged in the kinds of activities that will enhance and fulfill their lives.

THE DIFFICULT PURSUIT OF NEW OBJECTIVES

In the preceding parts of this paper, I alluded to the Canadian aspect of the various problems under discussion, but only in the most general terms, with reference to the exceptional size of the country and the abundance of its re-sources. As we turn now to consider in somewhat greater detail the different steps along the road towards a more humane society in which resources are used in a rational manner, and the environment is respected, certain fundamental re-alities of the Canadian situation and the Canadian people need to be taken into account. The aims and objectives of a society cannot be defined solely at a global level. They must also include the indigenous social and cultural objectives of the specific communities that make up that larger society; it is impossible, except for the purposes of analysis, to treat these local objectives in isolation from the national ones. For if man manages to become integrated into large political units such as Canada, it is mainly through intermediate communities with their own characteristic qualities. And it is only within those smaller (and more natural) entities that men and women develop their full potential as individuals, within the framework of readily identifiable value systems, life-styles, and cultures.

With its five million French-speaking inhabitants, Quebec is an excellent ex-ample of such a community having an identity, a culture, and institutions of its own. The people of Quebec, by virtue of their cohesion, their numbers, and the stage of development they have reached, have all the attributes of a distinct society. There is nothing new about this fact: Lord Durham recognized it in

1838, and the union of Upper and Lower Canada was its official political expression. In 1964, shortly before the centennial of a confederation in which this reality had for all practical purposes been lost sight of, the Royal Commission on Bilingualism and Biculturalism once more drew attention to the existence of two distinct societies in Canada. Their preliminary report urged the recognition of this fact and concluded:

'More than most other countries, Canada is a creation of human will. It has been called a "geographical absurdity", an "appendage of the United States", a "4,000-mile main street" with many bare stretches. Nevertheless this country has existed for a long time, because its people have never stopped willing that there be a Canada.

'Each age is fascinated by the difficulties it must face; hence most generations go through periods of doubt. Present day Canada is no exception. But is it more difficult to maintain the entity of Canada today, to make necessary changes, than it was to create it yesterday?

'Canada will continue to exist, will grow and progress, will surmount the present crisis, if Canadians have the will – a will like that of the men who built the country.

'The present crisis is reminiscent of the situation described by Lord Durham in 1838: "I found two nations warring in the bosom of a single state." The circumstances today are very different; we have not just had a bloody revolt. On the contrary, one of the problems is that a part of the Canadian people does not realize that a gulf has opened, and that we have to rethink our partnership.

'The will we speak of cannot be stiff and arbitrary: it must take account of new circumstances. Like anything that is living it must constantly adapt to changing conditions. Above all, it must be based on awareness and understanding.

'The "negotiations" of which we spoke in the last chapter will be in large part the responsibility of the governments. We conceive them, however, also in a much larger sense. They concern the totality of the two societies in Canada. In our final report we hope, through our findings and recommendations, to make some contribution to the discussions and negotiations that must go on.'

Despite the authority and objectivity of the commissioners and the high context in which their analysis was formulated, their call went unanswered. As everyone knows, the 'negotiations' led to the Victoria Charter of June 1971. This document made no mention whatsoever of the existence of two societies or nations within Canada; instead, it stressed the need for a largely artificial pan-Canadian bilingualism for a highly centralized state. One need not therefore be surprised at the reception and fate of the Victoria Charter in Quebec.

This lack of understanding still persists today. As a result, many Québécois have given up any hope that Canada may one day live up to their aspirations. For the most part, it is unfortunately the younger people who take this attitude, those who in any society are usually responsible for change and progress. Not only Canada as a whole, but Quebec too in the present circumstances, is deprived of their creative energy; their beliefs arouse fear and apprehension among many of their fellow-citizens, who tend to reject their contribution to society, thus forcing them to adopt even more negative positions. Even for those who have not given up hope, the failure on the part of their fellow-Canadians to offer authentic recognition to the Quebec fact has given rise to a painful split in their loyalties: still wedded to the idea of Canada by their reason, in their hearts they sense that the rest of the country is a vehicle that may lead to the loss of their identity and to assimilation. Yet, torn as they are, their loyalty to Canada is none the less real, and it would be wrong to turn a deaf ear to their aspirations on the grounds that Canada seems to have weathered the crisis to which the commissioners referred. The mere absence of a crisis atmosphere hardly indicates that the problem has disappeared.

Despite the progress we have made in the last few years, we have not come to grips with the essential Canadian dilemma. French-speaking Canadians do play a more important role than hitherto, both in the federal government and in other Canadian institutions; but given the sheer number of French Canadians, this is hardly surprising. It is also true that economic development is moving ahead in Quebec, a fact that its citizens are the first to applaud, despite certain reservations about the way this development is being achieved. And in some areas of joint concern, where negotiations seemed formerly to have reached a stalemate, there now exist working arrangements between Ottawa, Quebec, and the other provinces which appear satisfactory to all parties. But these signs of progress, welcome as they are, do not indicate that the basic problem has been solved but merely that it is capable of solution.

From what I have said, it follows logically that a modification of our political structure, to bring it into line with certain facts of Canadian life and with the aspirations of the people, must be regarded as amongst the most urgent tasks ahead. The full implications of such a change are beyond the scope of this paper; but it nevertheless constitutes the essential background to any statements we make about the future, and therefore should be borne in mind as we turn, finally, to examine more closely some of the immediate objectives, specifically in the areas of population, political structures, and economic growth.

Towards a better population balance
In global terms, demographic growth presents no serious problem in Canada.

According to the most recent projections published by Statistics Canada, the long-term natural increase in population will be slow, due to the stabilization of the fertility rate at a low level. Given the vast extent of habitable land available these projections are not a cause for concern. However, merely because they are more fortunate in this respect than the people of many other nations, there is no reason for Canadians to conclude that demographic issues do not concern them. On the contrary, the very fact that we are not burdened with the more pressing problems associated with overpopulation gives us a moral responsibility to do everything in our power to help solve them in other parts of the world. At first sight, a generous immigration policy would appear to be the most positive contribution. But since this does not get to the heart of the problem of overpopulation, our efforts should take the form of increased aid to overpopulated countries in order to help them to achieve better living standards. It is becoming more and more apparent that a rise in the standard of living constitutes one of the most efficient and acceptable ways to curb population growth.

Moreover, we should not let our generally favourable circumstances – a small population in a very large country – blind us to the serious regional imbalances that, as far as one can judge from the most recent projections, seem likely to occur, most of them as a result of the errors of previous government policies. If the most realistic forecasts made by Statistics Canada prove to be accurate, it will be impossible to preserve a healthy social, cultural, and economic balance between the different regions, let alone between the two societies which make up the nation. By the year 2000, if current trends are maintained, 40 per cent of the population of Canada will live in Ontario, 23 (as opposed to the current 28) per cent in Quebec, 8 per cent in the Maritimes (instead of 9.5) and 5.5 (instead of 9) per cent in Manitoba and Saskatchewan. In the light of these figures, French-speaking Québecois may well wonder about their chances of survival as a distinct culture.

Clearly, our immigration policy should be revised as quickly as possible to rectify these imbalances. We also need to know much more about the underlying causes of emigration and internal migration, since these population movements are an important factor in the forecasts to which I have just referred. Only when such knowledge is available will governments be in a position to exert a positive influence on these movements. Regional development policies and programs have clearly a special role to play in this regard.

Since the preservation of some kind of equilibrium between the two populations making up the two communities is essential to national unity, Quebec must exercise a considerable initiative and responsibility in the formulation and implementation of policies affecting population trends. Only through this approach, which appears very reasonable, will Quebec be able to face up to the solution of its own problems and to restore confidence to its citizens who are at present beset by feelings of doubt and despair.

The modification of our political structures

Even though the objectives I have been discussing are based on the legitimate aspirations of the Canadian people, their formulation and implementation as a political program is bound to meet with considerable opposition, to which we might now turn our attention. In particular, we shall have to overcome the innate fear of change on the part of those who derive security from the existing order, even if it is far from perfect. The changes outlined in this paper will call into question sets of values to which many Canadians subscribe. The fact that they do so, in many cases, out of sheer force of habit will not make the changes any more palatable: the value placed on work for its own sake – the so-called Anglo-Saxon work ethic – is a case in point. The rate at which changes are introduced will have to be very carefully regulated if confrontations between generations and ideologies are to be avoided. Problems will also arise over the choice between different methods of reaching the stated objectives; the advantages and disadvantages of each, as well as their social and economic costs, will have to be weighed very carefully.

Fundamentally, these problems are related to three basic aspects of life in society, which may be put in the form of three questions: to what extent are individual citizens involved in determining objectives and ways of reaching them? How do they have access to the information required to participate in the decision-making process? And what are the political structures through which policies are determined and implemented?

As far as participation is concerned, I have already underlined its importance and suggested some of the forms it might take with respect to work. Participation is equally crucial in ensuring that the political structures in our society are kept to human dimensions, so that governments, by their size and degree of complexity, do not insulate themselves from individual citizens. Where this is not done, governments, while claiming to be democratic, in effect fall under the control of a handful of individuals and the interests they represent. Besides, participation appears to be the only way of introducing changes in a manner that is both orderly and democratic. For this reason, the inevitable setbacks, the delays, the costs in time and effort, and the difficulties of all kinds often associated with participation should be regarded as so many obstacles to be overcome in the pursuit of a society based on the association of all of its members.

It is impossible, within the limits of this paper, to examine in detail the necessary conditions without which participation will not work, or the various forms that it can take. Consequently, I shall simply draw your attention to the important role played by information in this regard; and second, to the fact that participatory democracy will only function within appropriate political structures.

Enormous strides have been made in the dissemination of information over the last few years, so that it is now possible to know about important or sensational events taking place anywhere in the world, while they are actually happening. By a curious paradox, it is hardly the sort of information that relates directly to the ordinary citizen, so as to provide him with what he needs to play his part in the political process. The sheer quantity of available information, much of it in the form of 'news' (and, too often, news of a sensational character) constitutes, by its very mass, an obstacle to the dissemination of such information. By the same token, the highly technical nature of many political issues – itself a consequence of the complex workings of our society – makes it extremely difficult to convey to the private citizen, at the right time and in readily understandable language, the information he needs to perform his civic duties. The task is complicated even further by the speed with which new, unforeseeable developments occur. Most of us are familiar, too, with the regrettable tendency on the part of administrative bodies to keep information to themselves, on the dubious grounds of confidentiality or increased efficiency: witness the city councils that sit in closed session or, if they do not, delegate their more important business to executive committees whose meetings are closed to the general public. In my view, this problem will not be solved by technological improvements: what is required is a change in political structures and mental attitudes.

Turning, then, to possible and desirable changes in those two areas, the first point to note is that Canada, like many other countries including our neighbour to the south, is committed to the path of centralization. Thus, municipal governments, by virtue of their failure to adapt their fiscal arrangements, their field of responsibilities, and even the physical boundaries of the districts under their jurisdiction, to the new realities of the urban environment, have seen their power progressively eroded. There is less and less correlation between the districts that fall, geographically speaking, under municipal government control, and the actual population distribution, particularly in rapidly urbanized agglomerations. Whereas municipal governments were originally set up with the purpose of regulating the immediate surroundings of their inhabitants, they no longer have adequate fiscal resources to carry out this task, and as a result are the easy prey of speculators and developers who, of course, operate with very different sets of objectives. Their financial weakness also leaves them open to provincial or federal intervention, reducing their power even more. Moreover there exists at the local and regional level a wide range of bodies created and funded by the federal or provincial governments and providing basic services in fields such as public transport, housing, sanitation, and police, bodies which are inevitably involved in the planning and organization of urban life; yet local governments have little or no say in determining either the policies or the programs of these bodies. What is even worse, these bodies in many cases do not come under any form of control by the citizens.

In these circumstances, it is hardly surprising that local governments fail to provide the leadership in civic affairs that is expected of them, or that the ordinary voter, increasingly conscious of this situation and of the fact that the decisions which really matter are taken at another level, is becoming more and more apathetic towards this area of political life.

The solution is all too clear. The responsibility of maintaining the fabric of our towns and cities and providing the services which correspond to the needs and wishes of the citizens must be given back to local administrations. In order to exercise this responsibility, these administrations must have access to adequate financial resources so that they are free to establish their own priorities. Those bodies at present controlled from the outside should either be put directly under local jurisdiction, or at least made subject to careful scrutiny by the local councils. Finally, their areas of responsibility should be set out much more clearly, in the light of contemporary realities, and left, as far as possible, to their exclusive jurisdiction. Only in this manner can the trend towards centralization be reversed, so as to allow urban development geared primarily to human needs, rather than to financial and economic interests. Secure in the knowledge of where the seat of power really lies – and of their access to it – private citizens will be able to play a positive role in the definition of their needs, and in the organization and administration of the services required to satisfy those needs; they will also be in a position to protect themselves more effectively against those whose interests run counter to their own. Finally, ethnic minorities will find an answer to their desire to preserve their cultural heritage, while at the same time being integrated into one of the two main linguistic and cultural streams that make up the nation.

It will be up to local governments to disseminate the necessary information with respect to their particular areas of responsibility; should they fail to do so, the voters will know where to put pressure in order to improve matters.

The current trend towards centralization of power may also be discerned at the provincial level, although for different reasons. Policies and programs of the provincial governments are highly concentrated in the service sectors. The cost of their operation grows at a faster rate than their fiscal revenues. Consequently, should a new situation arise, the provincial governments are forced to operate within very strict limits. In theory, they could give themselves more room to manoeuvre by raising the taxes; but the combined taxes already levied by the three different levels of government in most of the provinces are simply too high for this solution to be envisaged seriously.

The federal government, on the other hand, has for a number of years now enjoyed considerable freedom of action, thanks to the nature of its tax revenues, and the relatively lighter burden which, as the central government, it has to bear. It has not been slow to make use of this freedom, making its presence felt in every sector of public life, but especially in those areas where modern conditions have required new tasks to be performed, In fact, federal authority has been deployed in so many directions and in so many different ways that a considerable amount of research would be required before one could convey an adequate picture of just how and where it is currently felt. Still, the over-all situation is clear enough: it is the federal government that, increasingly, establishes priorities, decides policies, and the way those policies will be put into effect in all sectors of Canadian life, including those which officially fall under local or provincial jurisdiction. Using the inability of the constitution to deal with the realities of contemporary life as a pretext, and its unlimited power of spending as a lever, the central government is effectively doing all it can to speed up the process of centralization. I need hardly add that whenever it intervenes in matters that normally fall under local or provincial jurisdiction, it is invariably with the most unimpeachable motives, such as 'Canadian unity' or 'national interest.'

Centralization is in the process of transforming the nature of provincial governments; it also runs counter to the whole spirit of Confederation, thus compounding one of the principal weaknesses of that structure, namely the failure to give clear recognition to the existence, within Canada, of two distinct societies.

If Canadians really mean to face up to the challenge of the future, and create a society in which the potential of every citizen is able to flourish, it is imperative that this trend towards centralization be reversed. This can only be done in two ways: 1/by making available to the provinces fiscal revenues commensurate with their responsibilities; and 2/by altering the constitution in such a way as to recognize the existence of two societies within the Canadian whole and give each one the political latitude essential for its development, and, in the case of Quebec, for its survival. Such a revision of the constitution would logically entail much clearer delimitation of the powers of each level of government. It is up to the Quebec government to define, in a democratic way and much more carefully than hitherto, the areas for which it must formulate policy. Basically, the objective is to assure the survival and development of one of the two societies which coexist in Canada, the more vulnerable of the two. This demarcation of areas of responsibility is essential if other Canadians are to appreciate that Quebeckers are not seeking privileges, and that their demands, far from being extravagant, are based on specific and legitimate objectives and do not, in any case, pose a threat to the survival of the Canadian state.

Economic growth
Nothing that has been said here implies that Canada should turn its back on the principle of economic growth, with increased production of goods and services to meet the demand in domestic and foreign markets, and constantly improved productivity following in the wake of technological progress. However, the shifts in priorities which we have been discussing will bring changes; and while one cannot gauge their full implications, these changes will undoubtedly be a source of tensions and, at the same time, a severe test for our political system and the men running it.

Rational use of resources, systematic recycling, elimination or reduction of pollution-causing factors – these objectives, together with a controlled rate of technological change (so that the social costs of such change, to which up till the present virtually no attention has been paid, may be properly assessed), are bound to slow down economic growth as we know it, that is to say, when measured in terms of the gross national product. In industry, delicate readjustments will be required to compensate for the effects of lower profits or rising production costs brought about by new demands or new standards, as is already apparent in those industries directly affected by the fight against pollution.

As far as the changes in urban development are concerned, once they are geared no longer to the principle of growth for its own sake, but to the needs of the population, their effect on the economy as a whole cannot be accurately assessed. In the long run, one may suppose that better living conditions in rationally developed towns would prove less costly, economically and socially, than the kind of urban growth that we are witnessing at present. On the other hand, it is safe to assume that speculators and developers will fight every inch of the way to prevent the introduction of the controls and restrictions that rational urban development implies. One can also expect a host of problems concerning the location and operation of factories, which civic authorities in their drive to protect the environment will feel obliged to place under strict surveillance.

Since the new priorities in tomorrow's society will be aimed first and foremost at satisfying the needs of the population, working through decentralized political structures in a spirit of participatory democracy, we may look forward to an improvement in the quality of life in the community as a whole. However, since this improvement will not be primarily an economic one, and since a larger allocation of resources will have to be devoted to the tertiary sector, we are likely to see some painful readjustments in the functioning of the economy and, no doubt, loud protests from those who measure progress solely in terms of material wealth. In the area of income redistribution, for example, one only has to look at the very partial success achieved by the present social security system, despite society's best efforts to the contrary, to appreciate the difficulties that lie ahead. Indeed, opposition to progress will be all the more stubborn in that growth of material wealth will be slower and its redistribution more clearly felt.

All these difficulties stem from the central problem with which we are all too familiar: how does one change the established order of things in a democratic society made up of many different groups of people, often with widely divergent interests, particularly if gradual change (i.e., reform rather than revolution) is assumed to be the guiding principle? Even in the Canadian context, the obstacles in the path of change constitute a challenge of considerable magnitude. They become even more so, when we see them (as we must) in an international context. Competition between nations, interrelated economies, the rising demand for natural resources and food of which only certain countries are producers, the growth of multinational corporations over which national governments have no effective means of control, the economic cycle and inflation, and the increasing need to provide aid to the developing countries in the third world: all these factors effectively limit the freedom of individual governments (especially in the less powerful nations) to determine their own objectives and the ways of attaining them.

This review of the obstacles to progress brings us back to the basic principle of participation. For some observers, the problems immediately ahead are so immense that some sort of dictatorship will be required to solve them. I am convinced there is another way, and a better one. It is to open up the decision-making bodies which control our political, economic, social, and cultural activities to the people they were created to serve. Only by so doing will individual members of society be able to make a realistic assessment of their common objectives, in the full knowledge of the costs of each option and the restrictions it will impose on them. Only through participation, too, will politicians be forced to take a longer term and more global view of society, one on which their decisions as to the best means of accomplishing social progress can be based. Finally, and perhaps most important of all, participation represents a way of bringing about change without the violent upheavals of which contemporary history offers us only too many sorry examples.

A CHALLENGE APPROPRIATE TO CANADA

Looking towards the future in the light of the Club of Rome findings, in the Canadian context, I do not think any purpose would be served by simply slowing down the rate of economic growth. We enjoy a privileged position, thanks to our peculiar combination of abundant natural resources, vast territory, and a small population. Our existing political, social, and economic structures give most of our citizens a standard of living and a measure of individual freedom which compare favourably with those of any other nation in the world. And we are fortunate enough to stand largely apart from the principal power blocs which struggle for ideological and economic world dominance, a position which, since the last world war, has enabled us to play a useful role as a mediator between the major world powers and an arbitrator in times of conflict.

It is this combination of circumstances that gives Canadians the chance, indeed the moral obligation, to adopt a positive, forward-looking attitude towards the challenge of the future. Working through democratic structures such as participation and decentralization, we must set ourselves new objectives, to be defined in terms of human needs (and not simply as by-products of economic growth). The task of reaching these goals will be a joint one, in which every citizen will have his part to play both as an individual and as a member of one of the two societies which constitute our nation. Apart from reducing the paralysing internal tensions and high social costs which plague us at the moment, the adoption of such a policy would enable Canada, with the wholehearted backing of Quebec, to become an example to those other nations who are looking for a better future than the one proposed either by the Russian brand of socialism or the American-style consumer society.

How new can it really be?

VIVIAN RAKOFF

Perennial man and the slowed machine

Everything seems uncertain and unpredictable and there is a general preoccupation with the future ranging from thoughtful disquiet to apocalyptic hysteria – a future which looks as if it may be disastrous if we don't get a grip on the diminishing resources and the dangerous inequities of 'space-ship earth.' The extreme version declares that it is already too late and many minor Noahs have retreated to building arks.

But who can accurately imagine the future? Can we bring to mind a single accurate prophet, someone who, apart from a sporadic flash which we retrospectively salute, has conjured a complete sequence of actions, let alone something as vast as the gestalt of an entire culture, or the interlocking of many cultures? In particular, the visionary prophets who inform our time seem to have been in all particulars wrong, although their emotional vision may persist. It is Marx's evocation of the horrors of early capitalism in his chapter on the working day, rather than his economic charts, which still seize the imagination of more than half the world. He was quite simply wrong in his predictions concerning where communism would first triumph and who would make revolutions and there is considerable room for debate about his theories of increasing misery and the capacity of capitalism to transform itself. Nevertheless his indignation and the hope he may have given to the oppressed has provided a polemical framework for change. In his recent *The Fascist Persuasion in Radical Politics,* A. James Gregor records that Mao had read very little Marx at the point he declared himself a Marxist; similarly Castro dismissed Marx's theory early on, declaring that one became a Marxist in action.

And the spiritual grandfather of this meeting, Malthus, has been wrong in almost every detail of his serious predictions – which is not to deride the direction of his concerns: we are after all launched on this subject because of Malthusian anxieties. Particular and more modest prophecies of technological changes in an imagined near-future have not been much better. Recently I read a complaint directed at *Popular Mechanics* for having promised so many simple things that never happened: we are not all landing on our roofs in private helicopters.

But there is at least one extraordinary historical prophecy, which fits the purpose of this paper in so far as it has polemical intention: De Tocqueville, writing in the first half of the nineteenth century before the American Civil War and before the Russian Revolution, prophesied that in the next century (ours) the world would be influenced by and divided between two powers, America and Russia. At that time they stood, as he said, in the wings of history, but their growing power was apparent. The statement is prescient enough as it stands, but De Tocqueville went on to anticipate in broad outline the institutions by which this power would be exerted: the Russians would continue to govern with central control, the Americans would continue to operate from a basis of small associations and would struggle with nature.

Of course, this short passage contains many questions and is open to all kinds of interpretation. But De Tocqueville's central vision of the unfolding of power in characteristic fashion within existing political institutions despite two unanticipated national cataclysms – the American Civil War and the Russian Revolution – remains valid. De Tocqueville's vision of the future was no more than a restatement of what he saw about him when he wrote.

All prophecy is essentially an elaboration of the present. Even the wildest science fiction or the most frivolous fantasizing must derive from the given. The invention of new forms or new modes of doing anything is rare and difficult. It appears to be a human characteristic that we always perceive and create on the foundation of received forms. In as restricted a field as the development of new forms in painting E. H. Gombrich has argued there is a marked consistency in history. And in the complicated matter of social forms, it would be impossible to project a future if we postulate a totally disruptive discontinuity. Any attempt to extrapolate the future of human life must take into account not only the history of a particular society, its great clusters of power and money and received political institutions, but also the phylogeny of the race itself. It is an intimidating exercise since it must assess and differentiate between those things one believes to be more or less constant factors of every human experience, and those which are dependent upon transient forces.

Let me start with here and now. We are gathered in the dining hall of Massey College which is the concretization of a European memory. Its particular history and its physical form goes back to at least medieval times. It expresses the structure of a community of scholars, who in addition to studying together, ate together and lived together. (Until very recently it also expressed a monastic tradition.)

Then to extend the boundaries: we are in prosperous Canada; the second largest land mass in the world, with over twenty million people, an advanced industrial society with abundant resources. And we are here in an envelope of a tradition powerful enough to cross an ocean, to survive separation from the generative stream and to grow again in physical and moral form. We are in short, a laboratory demonstration that there is a continuity in human affairs, which reflects a fundamental psychological capacity and need. In spite of its almost apocalyptic subject matter, this occasion has some grace. It takes place in an ambience which I guess approaches luxury. And there is an aspect to it which suggests an elaborate game: we must consider a Canada beyond industrial growth; Canada not Africa, not India or Brazil. Furthermore, this highly serious game presupposes that we have choice and that we can choose to limit industrial growth. We suppose that our huge larder of resources will still be relatively full.

Out there it is different and we must realize that there is a world where the larder is often nearly empty. It will make demands on us and it may generate precisely that cataclysm which may make this series of lectures irrelevant and stupid – but I hope not heartless.

If we don't recognize that other world, we *will* be both heartless and foolish. 'Beyond growth' may not be a choice for them. At the recent world conference in Sweden on pollution and industrial growth, certain Third World powers suggested – we don't know how seriously – that attempts to halt industrial growth were perhaps a plot of the developed capitalist world to prevent them from achieving something even slightly approaching the standard of living which many of us in the West would already regard as inadequate. The Brazilians, for example, are cynical not only about concepts of personal liberty as defined in Canada, but about our concerns that global oxygen supplies may be related to the integrity of their huge Amazonian forests. Our concerns do not move them: the global atmosphere will not be preserved at the expense of their economic backwardness.

But we must hope that in the end some choice may still be ours, in spite of nightmares such as nuclear blackmail. And let us accept the premise that we will be able to contain ourselves for a while in some kind of *cordon sanitaire*. (After all, without the handkerchief there would be no Othello; if the messenger had arrived, Romeo and Juliet need not have died.) Let us assume that we in Canada do in fact have the choice of husbanding our resources and – most crucially – that, while we recognize a variety of possible disasters, we will adjust to them in accordance with our received history, a history that is both a psychological and political heritage. A cataclysm is not included in these premises, but the threat of cataclysm is. We must anticipate as an additional premise a constant threat to our body politic as it excites envy among poorer people.

But men have always lived under threat. In that regard, we are and will be no different from any previous generation. In spite of our apparent need to believe that we live in the most difficult time ever, this may simply reflect a kind of perverse historical narcissism. Beyond the walls of Athens there were barbarians; the Vikings could sail up the estuary at any moment; the Great Wall girdling the Middle Kingdom kept generations busy; and the Turks did come to the gates of Vienna. And above all, death is a perennial reality. No human being has ever lived without the threat of annihilation from some source.

But if there is global nuclear war, then socio-political history as we know it may arrive at a sudden horrible discontinuity. Not an end, for if there is only one Noah and his wife surviving, the story we are concerned with this evening will continue. As long as the survivors have human psyches, minds, souls, and human anatomy, they will be recognizably our historical kinsmen.

For this occasion let us assume there may be trouble, even great trouble, but not big enough trouble to destroy this somewhat strung out and tenuous body politic of Canada. We have reason to hope that we will continue to be Canadians in our own curiously undefined way. There is evidence that historical continuity is very difficult to disrupt. In the world at this moment, as Glazer and Moynihan pointed out in a recent article in *Commentary* (Oct. 1974) there is an unexpected persistence of ethnic communities with a tenacious grip on their identity and a profound feeling for perennial rights. Admittedly, there are people who have disappeared as entities, and great national traditions have perished. It is obvious there is no persistence of Periclean Athens in Greece; everyone can recite a litany of vanished glories. However, our task is to anticipate not the remote science fiction world of millenia hence – we are looking at the day after tomorrow. Earlier I referred to De Tocqueville's extraordinary prediction not only of the roles of the United States and the Soviet Union in this century, but also his guess that their political modes would endure. It is not the whole truth, but it is interesting that China, probably the most revolutionary society of our time – China which has consciously and at times brutally rejected a past devoted to Confucian maxims and to gerontophilia – China is now governed by a powerful, self-sustaining gerontocracy, has a famous source of maxims, and greedily pursues the boundaries of the Middle Kingdom. One may tentatively say that forms persist, but content changes. If we adopt an optimistic scenario, the same will hold true for Canada – a Canada where our fairly consistent concern with more or less social justice, more or less rule of law, more or less pluralist institutions, in a climate of appalling winters, will continue. We are already launched into a more or less welfare state, and although there are pockets of social injustice and lack in our country, we generally eat enough or too much. Our sense of what constitutes poverty may be laughable in some parts of the world, and we expect health, education, and housing as some kind of a right.

In terms of political history, this is not Zaire or Bangladesh or Albania contemplating a slow-down of the huge machine; this is essentially humane Canada stretching almost by accident from sea to sea. Politically we are formed by the somewhat warped but continuing institutionalized mythology of the British political tradition. But before we retreat from that as good Canadian pluralists, take comfort that that myth in turn derives from Jewish, Christian, Greek, and Roman ingredients, recombined in that protected island, into a uniquely pragmatic and humane political tradition.

I must make it clear that I regard myths as more powerful than bombs. The 'myth' in Levi-Strauss's terms is the great sense-making structure of human societies. Myths determine where bombs will fall. But we have a tradition which is not unself-conscious or subliminally primitive. In spite of monstrous back-sliding, we have been actively aware of some magnetic poles of aspiration which have given the political history of Canada a constant if erratic development toward greater democracy.

In the end, if we achieve the steady state, it will look very much like today in many of its important aspects. Furthermore, I will assume that some present currents at work in our political life will have developed further. Along with the rights to education, health, and housing I have already mentioned, I will assume more equitable distribution of income: some ceiling above which no one will be able to earn, and a guaranteed minimum income. And since our central premise is a restriction of industrial growth, we may presume that the work week will shrink considerably and for many it may hardly exist at all.

Economically at least, the prospect is not Malthusian gloom. We have the possibility of a population sufficiently fed, with some work, but with energies not fully absorbed by labour and with more time for other activity. Let us simply say there will be time, but as in the past and in the present we will continue to be plagued by the problems inherent in our given humanity.

THE FREUDIAN LEFT

Up to now I have been emphasizing continuity. The emphasis on historical continuity has been a psychological rather than a political one, in the sense that the political structures reflect the underlying social mythologies which all societies have and which are the societal equivalent of an individual's experience of his own identity. Identity is fundamentally the experience of one's own continuity, that thread which allows one to say, shown the pictures of a baby, a boy, a middle-aged man, and an old white-haired man, 'Oh, that is William Thackeray.' I have laboured this point, but it has consequences necessary to the particular polemic I am advancing. And this is frankly a polemical paper.

The polemic is directed explicitly against some current formulations of human aspiration which hold out the hope of a new man who will arise when we are freed from the restraints of contemporary 'capitalist imperialist' society. They hold that the psychological relationships of most men are explicitly linked to contemporary socio-political sources and do not reflect perennial social, or more importantly, psychological endowment. A discontinuity of human personality is not only believed to be possible; it is welcomed as a goal – a revolutionary goal. Those who express these views imagine a radical transformation of human characteristics that some of us regard as essential human attributes beyond time and culture. I am referring to those thinkers included in what Paul Robinson has called the Freudian Left: Wilhelm Reich, Geza Roheim, Herbert Marcuse, and among others Norman O. Brown, Ronald Laing, and David Cooper. There are also several minor figures who variously suggest similar goals through religious revival, drugs, exercises for the transformation of consciousness, astrology, diet, or (at its wildest) superstitious hopes of an invasion and hence a redemption by invaders from outer space.

It is difficult not to caricature these thinkers. Robinson says of Roheim, Marcuse, and Reich that they were 'Injudicious ... they harbour only contempt for the pluralistic tolerance of the liberal imagination ...' He goes on to say that he admires them for their capacity to pursue radical ideas to even preposterous limits, and that he rejects Weber's idea of a *wertfrei* or value-free science, even as an aspiration. But then he was writing in Stanford in 1968 and 1969.

Although Roheim, unlike Reich and Marcuse, rejected Marxism, he shares with them the rejection of Freud's conception of civilization as the product and indeed the prize of the inevitable conflict between desire and repression. For all of them, the repressive aspect of the perennial conflict is not only unnecessary but a violation of human possibility. All civilization for Roheim is a castrating device to keep men safely infantilized. Without its restrictive structures, man – and his prime examples are the Australian aborigines – would be released into a non-terrified genitality. Politicians and politics, in Roheim's view, whatever their stamp, are simply extreme agents of the repressive infantilizing forces inherent in the body politic.

Wilhelm Reich too expounded a personal anthropology which derived principally from rethinking Freud's great oedipal myth, not through careful field work, but through intellectual elaboration based upon his perception of case histories. The sequence of murders and totemic feasts of the primal horde was reconstructed in consulting rooms in Vienna and the United States. The watershed of human trouble in Reich's formulation was the point at which permissive, orgasm-encouraging, maternal social organization gave way to repressive paternalistic anti-sexual patterns. The goal for free man in a free society is for Reich the complete orgasm, which represents not only personal freedom but is in addition the product of social freedom. Politics and sexuality were intimately linked; the sexual revolution was to be linked to the political revolution.

Marcuse is probably the most subtle of this group. He is a classical German Hegelian-Marxist and he has described himself as a romantic. He is also frankly utopian, believing that there should be no limit to human aspiration. At his most extreme he even denies that we have to accept the idea that death is inevitable. He argues that, by breaking down the power of the father and the family organization, the state has become incorporated into the individual's unconscious. There is no longer within the developed capitalist state a barrier between the individual and the repressive constricting forces of the society. Since the state is part of the structure of his super-ego, he cannot readily judge it or easily rebel against it. His instinctual and specifically his sexual life are rejected in favour of his utilitarian performance. And the performance principle has resulted in surplus repression until the individual is left with only the shell of his human possibility. The state does allow in restricted ways access to libidinal satisfaction which may appear to be sexually satisfying, but this release is only allowed in ways which in the end keep the victim a little more contented within his socio-economic prison. He is not allowed access to true joyous and if necessary explosive and destructive expression of instinctual need, but may be cooled off by a process of repressive desublimation through access to pornography and the like. In making social revolution Marcuse urges that radical and defiant modes of conduct should be adopted.

In *Eros and Civilisation* he endorses Schiller's aesthetics, for he realizes that the modes of play and self-expression are an essential aspect of man's social being. One hesitates to suggest that those signs of the late sixties' counter-culture, the frisbee and rock music, have their roots in Schiller's aesthetics. If they don't they most certainly fit Marcuse's description of it: an aesthetic of Orphic enthusiasm with few rules, sensual, emotional, and frankly erotic. In all this there is a new man who will relate more passionately and more freely in what he calls an affirmative culture. Marcuse, the somewhat difficult thinker, the reasoner, rejects reason, neutrality, and respect for facts. His swear word is 'liberalism.' For liberalism is the enemy of true freedom and, at least at one point in his career, he explicitly praised destructive behaviour as something desirable. (He has much to be responsible for.) It is precisely the world we have been imagining in which Marcuse sees the possibility for the coming into being of his new Orphic man: a society with an advanced but orderly economy, where men are freed from the daily struggle for bread and in which they have time.

More radical, and for me personally more difficult to follow, than any of the above is Norman O. Brown, who also imagines a new man freed by technology towards a liberated conception of true humanity. Reichian genitality, the sensual freedom of Roheim, the elaborate playful eroticism of Marcuse are not enough for Brown. Reich specifically elevates the genital heterosexual orgasm to the status of ultimate good, and Marcuse at best regards the homosexual as a species of social critic, whereas Brown holds that limitation of sexuality in any way at all is repressive and counter-human and is the result of the death-affirming hate-filled forces of society. True liberation will consist of a return in adult life to a state of infantile polymorphous perversity. He writes in *Love's Body*: 'To heal is to make whole, as in wholesome, to make one again; to unify or re-unify: this is Eros in action. Eros is the instinct that makes for union or unification and Thanatos the death instinct, is the instinct that makes for separation or division ...' Later he says, 'To make in ourselves a new consciousness, an erotic sense of reality ...' 'Sleepers awake,' he exhorts. 'Sleep is separateness; the cave of solitude is the cave of dreams, the cave of the passive spectator. To be awake is to participate, carnally and not in fantasy, in the feast, the great communion.' To read Brown is difficult for me, but every now and again a hortatory flash connects and I think I understand something of his conception of unity in which everything is transformed into everything else, and sexuality is seen as a pentecostal flame melting all contraries into redemptive fusion. And having just said that, a commonsense deflator makes me recoil, for looking about me in the real world I see no precursors of this possibility.

By comparison Ronald Laing, who exhorts us to be a little madder than we are and to have respect for varieties of experience which our ordinary rationalism precludes, is, in the company of these thinkers, far from radical. He only wants us to open ourselves to new experiences. It is true that in *Reason and Violence* he aligns himself with Sartre, but it is probably Sartre at his most conservative: the Sartre who promulgates a view of the group as a collection of mutually tyrannical individuals. In the end Laing pleads for psychic charity, not the revolution, although he too holds up a glimpse of a new man in a new society who is somewhat more orgiastic than today's constricted universal consciousness seems to allow.

David Cooper wants more than Laing, but his vision, when it is clear, is in a different direction. For Cooper the essential repressive instrument of society is the family. Whereas Marcuse sees the disappearance of the protective old paternalistic family as facilitating the repressive state, Cooper sees the family as the paradigm for all the state's repression. It both tyrannizes the individual members and at the same time protects them under the guise of a spurious benevolence from experiencing essential aloneness and guards them from necessary suffering.

Cooper makes explicit one thread which is more or less implicit in the others, the aloneness of the individual. As Sonya Rudikoff, reviewing *Death of the Family*, remarked, 'It is a recipe for a very lonely old age.'

While these utopian visionaries have much to say about the relationship of the erotic to the political system, their conception of the nature of the individual is not clearly defined. There is much of eroticism, but the anthropology is a private mythology and the notions of family, society, and community are very sketchy.

The apocalyptic radical thinkers develop an individual with few social bonds beyond his essential eroticism. Other forms of bonding in Roheim and Reich are reduced to anthropological fantasy, although, to be fair to Marcuse, he has said that he liked the park benches in Hanoi because they are so small that only two people can sit on them at a time. And having achieved his particular blend of Marx and Freud he conceived of the tight relationship which exists between an analyst and his patient as one of the few truly human relationships possible at this time.

For all its emphasis on erotic, sensuous freedom, orgasmic joy, playfulness, mystic polymorphism, the over-all model these thinkers give us in various shadings is, at least for me, incomplete. Despite all the passionately espoused humanism of the radical apocalyptics, the man they conjure has been dehumanized into a rhetorical cipher. It provides the paradigm for terrorism, in which the victim is selected for his metaphorical not his actual attributes. The world of the experience is reduced, in the most dangerous way, in favour of aesthetic expectations: a desire that existence should have the symmetry and symbolic significance of a work of art. And specifically it isn't Apollonian or tragic art, but the art of Orphic abandon, so that violence becomes mere theatre; blood is a colour, murder a gesture. The wish in the most infantile way becomes the sole arbiter of the ethical value of an action.

Norman Cohn in his great examination of the cults of enthusiasm in the late middle ages in *The Pursuit of the Millenium*, gives many examples of similar thinking, derived from antinomian theological premises rather than political psychological premises. 'Orthodox and heretical mysticism alike sprang from a craving for immediate apprehension of a communion with god; both alike stressed the value of intuitive and particularly of ecstatic experiences ... adepts of the free spirit were intensely subjective ... they believed that they had attained a perfection so absolute that they were incapable of sin.' In practice this led to promiscuity in principle. Referring specifically to the Armenian group of Euclites, wandering holy men, he says, 'They cultivated a self-exaltation that often amounted to self-deification and an antinomianism that often expressed itself in anarchic eroticism.' The quintessential statement is that of the mystic heretic Konrad Schmid: 'The truly free man is king and lord of all creatures. All things belong to him and he has the right to use whatever pleases him. If anyone tries to prevent him, the free man may kill him and take his goods.'

The questions I address to proponents of the new man in a new society come to me in very simple ways. Do you mean we will spend all day singing, dancing, and copulating? But what if I am not particularly beautiful, or I am aging and infirm, or if I have tastes which would only not be unusual to Norman O. Brown? Who will share them with me? What of the painful lack of reciprocity in unrequited love? What of my own failures of talent or intellect or kindness? How in short, will people in the flesh, not invented by non-empirical anthropology or the dream fantasies of politically preoccupied psychoanalysts or other near mystical thinkers, survive in the living of day to day? If we are to adumbrate models for the near future then surely they must come from some dimension of experience rather than bewildering speculation. In this model there should be some element of what David Riesman, responding to the rhetoric of the late sixties, called the 'daily' - everyday experience which takes so much of the time of ordinary flesh and blood people.

THE RIGHT TO PERSONALITY

There has been a model. Like all models it is not exactly concordant - there are elements which don't quite fit - but nevertheless it contributes to our projection into a leisured future. It is not a mass model and up to now it certainly is not a democratic one. I refer to the kind of life led by the lesser aristocracy of, say, the nineteenth century. Not the great nobles afflicted with great power, but the landed gentry who had more than enough to eat, who were relieved of having to perform hard regular labour and who had time to be concerned with their erotic lives, their moral lives, and their entertainments. Perhaps as a result of this amount of time, their lives did not generally turn into a formless blur - apart from some specifically institutionalized periods spent at university, school, in the army, or travelling. Rather, most activities became highly ritualized. One dressed in a prescribed costume for a given event; eating was ceremonialized; gaming behaviour required considerable ceremony; and social and erotic behaviour existed within elaborate etiquette. Ritual not only gives comfort, it adds significance, and the events of daily life acquire what may be a spurious significance. Given time and the release from pressing necessity, men invent ceremony.

This example may appear very strange, but it is not so extraordinary. For some time now, at least since the end of the Second World War, there has been a democratization of the aristocratic options. These options aren't completely encompassed in the idea of leisure time which carries connotations of holiday. Holiday and leisure can't be equated with the notion of a life essentially devoted to the expression of personality and the cultivation of social relationships. It isn't time out we are referring to, but a new mode of existence which does not constantly define itself in terms of work done or work avoided.

Once political rights as expressed by suffrage and certain fundamental social rights were more or less universally accepted in our society, a new series of social demands, which it would be difficult to define as specifically political or psychological, followed. Equal opportunity employment, the diminution of institutionalized racism, the extension of rights to women and so on are political rights, but their effect is profoundly psychological. They accumulate into the demand for freedom to express personality which has been for so long implicit in our political structure. (In an essay in *Sincerity and Authenticity* Lionel Trilling traces the process by which sincerity has become a particularly contemporary form of virtue. While honesty has always been a virtue, sincerity carries overtones of a truth to the self, a personalized form of honesty. At times the fact that behaviour is sincere is adduced as a virtue in itself.) The expression of personality has been elevated to a social good. Personality has, in the political sense, always been a luxury available only to the powerful, and not necessarily a pleasant luxury. It is a difficult taste to acquire – a kind of existential caviar.

In our chosen scenario there will be an increase in the opportunities for the discovery and assertion of personality. This is a grand phrase that requires some definition: the right, one might say, to determine the course of one's life and to affect events about one in accord with endowment and desire. In the theological sense there has always been a democracy of the soul in the expectation that one could choose between the virtuous however defined and the wicked however defined – a sense of standing naked and equal before god. Heaven, I suppose, was a democratic institution. But personality, in the sense we are addressing it, is a different dimension of individuality.

It is reflected in the literary forms of the western world. The right to conflict as it is related to character has been reserved for those with political and social freedom, with time to make decision out of choice and not always out of pressing necessity. It will be immediately clear that tragic choice was at first reserved for kings and nobles; the heroic was rarely a democratic attribute. Kings and queens and smaller nobility filled serious literature almost entirely until the beginning of the capitalist era. The poor – servants, porters, nurses, watchmen, guards, innkeepers – were comical. Their lives lacked density and weight, their suffering was not as real as the suffering of their betters. In the hands of genius, this tension produced a moral commentary on the preoccupations of the privileged, but it was a commentary upon the lives of those who were central to their own dramas by those who would always be attendant to a central action – who by social circumstances were always to be minor characters in the drama of someone else's life. Examples are Sancho Panza, Lear's fool, and the parallel plebian dramas in Shakespeare's histories.

With the bourgeois revolutions there was a bourgeois literature. In the nature of things the stream had become broader. There were more bourgeoisie than nobles and the nineteenth-century novel celebrated the assumption of the attributes of personality by the bourgeoisie. Hauptmann's 'Weavers' was a revolutionary play, not only because it was concerned with social protest but because it was a play about workers, not comical but asserting their right to personal existence. It was not until after the First World War that a travelling salesman was addressed with tragic intention (whatever one may feel about the success with which this was achieved). And lately groups – classes within classes – have demanded social recognition of their particular identity beyond comedy and beyond stereotype.

Among the serious demands of those groups has been the demand for correct naming. It may seem that the name changes demanded by blacks and women – no more niggers, no more girls – were frivolous touchiness or a kind of strident social paranoia. However, if this is perceived as a step towards proper social definition, both by self and others, and a demand for centrality, it becomes understandable within the historical framework of the broadening of the right to personality.

And the young in a confused and uncomfortable way have taken to themselves and demanded from society as a mass option modes of action reserved for young gentlemen of a century ago. They make the grand tour – hitchhiking it's true; but it isn't the mode of transport that is important so much as the feeling that it is perfectly all right to take off a year to see the sights and to discover how it is to be among strangers. Perhaps the situation in the universities is not as revolutionary as it seemed only a little while ago. Students have often been difficult, riotous, impossible. The university, it is true, was there always principally to allow scholarship. At the same time, it also provided shelter for young aristos who were practising their erotic skills, learning the art of politics, card-playing, hunting, debate, and play-acting. It was always an instrument of socialization toward a dominant norm. In our time the numbers are bigger. There are more young gentlefolk, in the oldest sense of the word, than ever before in history. Sowing of wild oats was never pretty and, lacking institutionalized form in the mass, it has been at times very frightening. But at least one of its curious aspects was that, while it seemed so new and threatening to the very structure of the university, it was in some ways very much within a perennial tradition. It was not one that would have made its central actors proud, but unconsciously their assertion of right assumed the safety of their world about them in the university. They were young lordlings behaving wilfully, testing their wings within the lavish playground their parents and their parental proxies in the state and university had built them. This is not entirely to deflate the high seriousness of their intentions; but it may be helpful to place them within a tradition. This Eriksonian moratorium has become in America almost a biological stage of development, and it is difficult to remember that the social aspects of adolescence used to be the rare privilege of the privileged.

The expansion of these privileges can be expected to continue beyond industrial growth. Groups of the population not yet validated by a manifest social struggle, such as blacks and women, will want similar things for themselves. How will it be when the population is larger and not necessarily well educated, or moderately well educated, or rich? What will we do with our days to fill time, to give our lives significance? What kind of people will we be?

OF HUMAN BONDING

Although it has been suggested that alienation is directly related to the freedom of movement within relatively prosperous democratic societies, the degree of our alienation will nevertheless be limited by our human givens. The family may change its form, but there is no human society without the family; and since a considerable amount of physical movement has been directly related to the demands of a rapidly expanding economy, an economy of stasis will probably inhibit the restless travelling of the postwar years. By simply staying closer to one another we may produce the end of the nuclear family as our primary social unit. Not in Cooper's sense of exploding it into an apocalyptic carnival, but in its transformation to an older form of extended family. There are dimensions to our history beyond those to which I have already referred: the history of our given humanness, a psychobiological coding which we don't fully understand but which must account for common human preoccupation and need extending throughout time and common to most cultures. For we bond to one another in community because of inescapable attributes and because of ethological endowment; and our community embraces generations. So that in however extreme a fashion we conjure a utopia or a near utopia, we will remain within what we have always been in many essential ways. The direction of our happiness or unhappiness will continue to be determined by the manner in which we come to terms with our wishes or desires: and it doesn't matter that we will have grander wishes or desires, or needs commensurate with a new-found sense of our own worth.

Even Marcuse's limit-defying radicalism is postulated on a well-functioning society with enough supplies to make a human life possible. Such a society will inevitably be a complex one with social tensions constantly at play. It is precisely such a society as will have made a conscious decision to inhibit its potential for growth and will have renounced its economic drive that will require Freud's vision in *Civilization and Its Discontents* rather than Marcuse's *Eros and Civilization*. It will be in the most classical sense a society caught in the Freudian vision of the tragic in both the personal and social dimensions. If ever a civilization will have been the product of the constant denial of impulse at the economic level, this will be it. But while this may be an inescapable part of our imagined future, it is not radically different from the conditions which social man in some way or other has always had to endure. In spite of the radical models I discussed earlier, there is nowhere a human society which remotely approaches them and their orgiastic self-celebration; such societies are invariably but Rousseauistic fantasies.

In place of the anthropology of Roheim and Reich, we have evidence of a loose kind derived from the folk stories, mythologies, and the literature of numerous societies which suggests that there are continuing variables common to all humanity and not generated by the structure of the capitalist nation-state. These accumulated tales are a body of informal anthropology which underline that mankind recognizes love, ambition, envy, happiness, despair, parenthood, childhood, and an obsession with the need to make sense of existence.

It is foolish to imagine that most men in the future will be more cerebral or philosophical or, on the other hand, more heartless than their predecessors. They will still be afflicted by the appeals of unreason and the frivolities of fashion as they have been in the past. For example, when Charles Taylor, in a previous essay, considered the planning of the economy, he suggested that there would still be choice among goods and I have no reason to suppose that the preoccupation with costuming will be less.

The question remains: what will we *do* in the homeostatic future? Apocalyptic visions always ignore this question in favour of grand schemata which are, like the heroic architecture of the fascist era, not meant for non-polemical living. But daily routine, of getting up in the morning, of struggling and communicating with more or less consistent figures, having meals more or less on time, brushing one's teeth, changing one's clothes and bed linen, are in fact the great and necessary and invisible envelope inside which we will continue to live our lives.

The relatively new science of ethology suggests that we are in the grip of biological history to an extent that most of us had not appreciated. And our attachments define our individuality as essentially embedded in social context with necessary and valued other persons. We know from studies of attachment behaviour in small children and from the response that babies have to the adult face and that adults have in turn to the baby's smile, that we are locked perhaps beyond volition to one another. This is only an additional and 'more scientific' extension of the informal anthropology to which I previously referred. But our bonding is probably most displayed in the compulsiveness of our sexuality; in their emphasis upon it, the radicals are probably correct. The Reichian orgasm, however, does not totally involve the partner, and the freedom in Brown's and Laing's vision is, for the experiencing self, radical masturbation. This complex of connected others - one's place in society - is not given its proper and its human-izing weight. It seems to me, for example, that it would be foolish to anticipate that people will not be unhappily in love as frequently as now.

But having asserted that we will go on in fundamental ways much the same as we are at present, I think we must consider the ways in which we may be differ-ent. I would like to return to the concept of the aristocratic options to which I referred. What characterizes this behaviour is ritualization and playfulness. Play-fulness means structured behaviour which appears to have no immediate utili-tarian goal; some psychologists have labelled it the pursuit of mastery. And play-fulness is manifest in all elaborated human activity, principally in art, sexuality, and athletics - activities which imply available time and the valuing of the self. Art is probably the most elaborate form of playfulness available to us. While I am sceptical about the assertion that in the millenium every man will be an artist, probably more people will engage in activities which we now call artistic. But I imagine the geniuses and great innovators, whose work is both imaginative ex-tension and ethical commentary on our lives, will continue to be rare. And for the most part, just as today, artistic productions will be at best exercises in craft and at worst painting by numbers.

Given the time that will be available, the erotic may become as elaborately ritualized as it was during the period of the love courts. Very few people have the talent to write their own life scenarios, and erotic fashion is as dominant as any other form of fashion. I doubt if an entire culture will ever condone 'letting it all hang out,' and even if it pretends to do so, it will only do so in severely pro-scribed form. The ways in which one will express one's freedom from restraint - if that is the received mode - may be as proscribed as the uniforms of freedom which were fashionable very recently.

However, the most serious playfulness will probably be in the dominion of ethical concerns. Again for most people, the forms will be received from those who are both talented in and preoccupied with these matters. All forms of be-haviour contain their characteristic potential for corruption - the entropic form of the activity. The corruption of artistic playfulness is mere aestheticism or formlessness or self-indulgence. The corruption of sexuality is frozen formalism or a decadent weariness perpetually looking for novelty. The possible corruptions of the moral religious impulse are written into the histories of heresy hunting, religious warfare, and the cults of anomie and enthusiasm to which I have re-ferred and which have recurred in our civilization.

The ritual making of art and fashion are used to give shape and meaning to our moral existence in pleasing and satisfying ceremonial. However, if we remind ourselves of the threat of encircling deprived nations, there will always be the dangerous possibility, which we can already see, of a new 'failure of nerve.' The religious preoccupation, even for scientific men, can quickly decay into astrological guru-seeking superstition, in which there will be no more questioning, only grabbing for answers so universal and so absolute that they will answer all unasked questions now and in the future. Faith in a perfect arbitrary master, the search for omens, and the rejection of all questions in matters of faith, remain a terrible possibility. We must remember that the Catholic church at first rejected a belief in witchcraft as heresy, but a century later the church led the way in hunting out witches. Is someone – who looks very benign – at this moment writing a new *Malleus Maleficarum*?

But the greatest danger does not seem to be in considering (rather sadly perhaps) that in fundamental ways we will continue as we were. It is true that this point of view contains a danger of reactionary conservatism and a refusal to look for new forms and possibilities. But the greater danger in our century has been the recurring promise of a new man – the temptation of stepping out of history to create a radically different human being. The new man is rarely promised in societies we would describe as democratic. He is always promised by a restrictive society, and the new man is usually found in the rhetoric of a dictatorship. It is my simple central thesis that if we deny the phylogenetic and historico-psychological human endowment in a setting of consistent natural laws, we are open to Messianism – generally a disastrous option. The perfect master eventually becomes the only master.

A modest expectation of troubles of a different kind, with a little more dignity, may be anti-heroic, but may allow more personal heroism.

If recently we have been warned that we ignore instinctual man at our peril, Orphic enthusiasts should be reminded that we also ignore that other irrational dynamo – the super-ego, the conscience – at our cost. It may return more tyrannically in the guise of absolute freedom than in any other way.

In spite of my reservations concerning the heroic, I should like to finish with the words of a heroine. Nadezhda Mandelstam is the widow of the great Russian Jewish poet, Osip Mandelstam. For the forty or so years since his murder by Stalin, she has preserved his memory and his manuscripts through exile and persecution. She writes: 'To think we could have had an ordinary family life with its bickering, broken hearts, divorce suits. There are people in the world so crazy as not to realise that this is normal human existence of the kind everybody should aim at. What wouldn't we have given for such ordinary heartbreaks.'

This old woman, who believed briefly in her youth in the possibility of historical discontinuity, concludes: 'But it takes a very special kind of education to know this.'

What is 'beyond'?

GEORGE GRANT

'The computer does not impose on us the ways it should be used'

'Beyond industrial growth' can be interpreted with the emphasis on any of the three words. Different issues will arise depending upon which word is emphasized. My task in this series is to emphasize 'beyond.' What will it be like to live on the further side of industrial growth? The other day when I had taken a foreign guest to Burlington she asked me on our return to Dundas: 'Where is Toronto?' I replied: 'Toronto is on the further side of Burlington.' (What it is to be beyond Burlington is of course quite beyond my imagination.)

The thinker who first caught the dilemmas of our contemporary society called his chief exoteric book *Jenseits von Gut und Böse*, which we translate as *Beyond Good and Evil*. Nietzsche claimed to say what it is for human beings to be on the further side of good and evil. Taking a spatial preposition, he applied it to the temporal unfolding of events. So equally 'beyond industrial growth' concerns temporality. It raises for us the uncertainty of what it will be like to live in a future society the chief end of which will no longer be able to be industrial growth.

How will it be best to live in a society on the further side of industrial growth? Those of us who have been conscious of living in North America have known what it is to live within industrial growth. To grasp the pure essence of what is given in that 'within' would be in Canadian terms to recollect fully the rule of C. D. Howe. The uncertainty in 'beyond industrial growth' arises from having known what it is to live within it, while we do not know the passage of time to the future which will take us to live beyond it – if indeed we are intended ever to live on that further side.

The situation in which we find ourselves seems obvious: we are faced with calamities concerning population, resources, and pollution if we pursue those policies (here designated as industrial growth) which have increasingly dominated societies over the last centuries. The attempt to deal with these interlocking emergencies will require a vast array of skills and knowledge. Indeed it will probably take a greater marshalling of technological mastery to meet these crises than it took to build the world of industrial growth from which the crises now arise. This mastery will now have to concentrate around the conquest of human nature rather than around the sciences concerned with non-human nature, as was the case in the past. As Heidegger has said, the governing and determining science is inevitably going to be cybernetics.

In North America the government of this science will be increasingly carried out by the dynamically proliferating power of the medical profession. Already this profession has been given control over mass foetuscide, and is more and more an instrument of social control through the mental health apparatus. North American capitalism increasingly attempts to establish itself as the mental health state, with the necessary array of dependent sciences and arts. Beyond the vast list of new arts and sciences – which in their modern combination we call technologies – there will hopefully continue to be the political art. With its proper mixture of persuasion and force within and between nations, that political art is required if human beings are to deal sensibly with the immediate crises. The practical wisdom of politics was called by Plato the royal *techné* – that art which is higher than all particular arts because it is called to put the others in a proper order of subordination and superordination.

Clearly I am not presenting a paper in this series because of any expertise in the technologies. I have little knowledge of cybernetics. Certainly I have not the practical wisdom which should lie at the heart of politics. Being a practitioner neither of any particular technology nor of the royal *techné*, what are my credentials for speaking about these crises? Presumably my business concerns the place of 'values' and 'ideals' in these crises.

In the difficult choices which will be necessary if we are to adapt to a new view of industrial growth, it is assumed to be essential that we hold before us 'values' which shall direct our creating of 'history.' If we are to deal with this future humanly, our acts of 'free' mastery in creating history must be decided in the light of certain 'ideals,' so that in coming to grips with this crisis we preserve certain human 'values,' and see that 'quality of life' as well as quantity is safeguarded and extended in our future. For example, clearly the problem of coming to terms with industrial growth involves great possibilities of tyranny; we must therefore be careful that through our decisions for meeting this problem we maintain the 'values' of free government. In the 'ascent of life' which is our self-creation, we must see that we create a fuller humanity, a society of 'persons.' Because of our secularized Christian tradition of liberalism, there is always someone to ice the cake of technological necessity with some high-minded discussion of 'values' and 'ideals' in the midst of more careful talk about difficult techno-logical requirements. 'The question is not simply to solve the problem of indus-trial growth,' it is often stated, 'but to solve it in terms which will preserve and extend human values.'

Yet – and it is a long yet – as soon as such an account is given, it forces me to disclaim this kind of talk, Why? The way of putting the task - in terms of such concepts as 'values,' 'ideals,' 'persons,' or 'our creating of history' – obscures the fact that these very concepts have come forth from within industrial growth, to give us our image of ourselves from within that within. Therefore to be asked to think 'beyond industrial growth' is to be asked to think the virtue of these con-cepts. If we do not, the significance of the phrase 'beyond industrial growth' fades away into an unthought givenness.

To show that this is so is the purpose of this paper. This may seem a negative job in the light of all the practical things that need doing. Yet it is a necessary one. Nearly all our current moral discourse about technological society falls back to rest upon such unthought concepts as 'values' and 'ideals.' By so doing, it re-volves within the hard-rimmed circle of technological society and cannot issue in thought. The moral exhortations of our politicians, our scholars, our psychiatrists, our social scientists are caught in this circle, so that their words become a tired celebration of technological society. Therefore this negative task is a necessary preparation to anything positive which may lie beyond it.

I will carry it out by examining at length a statement by a man who works at making and using computers. He said: 'The computer does not impose on us the ways it should be used.' Similar statements are heard about other technical fields and are often generalized into statements about all technologies.

Obviously the statement is made by someone who is aware that computers can be used for purposes of which he does not approve, for example, the tyrannous control of human beings. This is given in the word 'should.' He makes a state-ment in terms of his intimate knowledge of computers which transcends that in-timacy in that it is more than a description of any given computer or of what is technically common to all such machines. Because he wishes to state something about the possible good or evil purposes for which computers can be used, he expresses, albeit in negative form, what computers are, in a way which is more than their technical description. They are instruments, made by human skill for the purpose of achieving certain human goals. They are neutral instruments in the sense that the morality of the goals for which they are used is determined outside them. Many people who have never seen a computer and almost certainly do not understand what they do, feel they are being managed by them and have an undifferentiated fear about the potential extent of this management. This man, who knows about the making and using of these machines, states what they are, so that the undifferentiated sense of danger is put into a perspective, freed from the terrors of such fantasies as the myth of Dr Frankenstein. The machines are obviously instruments because their capacities have been built into them by men, and it is men who must set operating those capacities for purposes they have determined. All instruments can be used for wicked purposes and the more complex the capacity of the instrument the more complex the possible evils. But if we apprehend these novelties for what they are, as neutral instruments, we are better able to determine rationally their potential dangers. That is clearly a first step in coping with these dangers. We can see that these dangers are related to the potential decisions of human beings about how to use computers, and not to the inherent capacities of the machines. Here indeed is the view of the modern scene I have been talking about and which is so strongly given to us that it seems to be common sense itself. We are given an historical situation which includes certain objective technological facts. It is up to human beings in their freedom to meet that situation and shape it with their 'values' and their 'ideals.'

Yet despite the decency and seeming common sense of the statement 'The computer does *not* impose on us the ways it should be used,' when we try to think what is being said in it, it becomes clear that computers are not being allowed to appear before us for what they are. To show this, I start from an immediate distinction. The negation in 'the computer does *not* impose' concerns the computer's capacities, not its existence. Yet clearly computers are more than their capacities. They have been put together from a variety of materials, consummately fashioned by a vast apparatus of fashioners. Their existence has required generations of sustained effort by chemists, metallurgists, and workers in mines and factories. It has required a highly developed electronics industry and what lies behind that industry in the history of science and technique and their novel reciprocal relation. It has required that men wanted to understand nature, and thought the way to do so was by putting it to the question as object so that it would reveal itself. It has required the discovery of modern algebra and the development of complex institutions for developing and applying algebra. Nor should this be seen as a one-sided relation in which the institutions were necessary to the development of the machines, but were left unchanged by the discovery of algebra. To be awake in any part of our educational system is to know that the desire for these machines shapes those institutions at their heart in their curriculum, in what the young are encouraged to know and to do. The computer's existence has required that the clever of our society be trained within the massive assumptions about knowing and being and making which have made algebra actual. Learning within such assumptions is not directed towards a leading out but towards organizing within. This entails that the majority of those who rule any modern society will take the purposes of ruling increasingly to be congruent with this account of knowing. In short, the requirements for the existence of computers is but part of the total historical situation (the word 'destiny' is too ambiguous to be employed at this point) which is given us as modern human beings. And the conditions of that situation are never to be conceived as static determinants, but as a dynamic interrelation of tightening determinations.

Obviously computers are, within modern common sense, instruments, and instruments have always been things which are made to be at human disposal. However, when the capacities of these machines are abstracted from their historical existence, and when their capacities are morally neutralized in the negative 'do *not* impose,' we shut ourselves off from what 'instrumentality' has now come to mean. For example, computers are one kind of technology. But just look at what is given in this very recently arrived word. Two Greek words, *techné* and *logos*, are brought together in a combination which would have been unthinkable till recently. The new word 'technology' is able to stand because it brings forth to us the new situation: a quite novel dependence of science upon art and a quite novel dependence of art upon science – in fact, a quite novel reciprocal relation between knowing and making. This novel relationship stands at the heart of the modern era. The simple characterization of the computer as neutral instrument makes it sound as if instruments are now what instruments have always been and so hides from us what is completely novel about modern instrumentality. It hides from us what we have to understand, if we are to understand industrial growth. The force of the negative 'do not impose,' as applied to computers, leads us to represent them to ourselves as if the instrumentality of modern technologies could be morally neutral. At the same time the very force of the computer as neutral raises up in the statement, in opposition to that neutrality, an account of human freedom which is just as novel as our new instruments. Human freedom is conceived in the strong sense of human beings as autonomous – the makers of their own laws. This also is a quite new conception. It was spoken positively and systematically for the first time in the writings of Kant. It is indeed also a conception without which the coming to be of our civilization would not have been. But it is a conception the truth of which needs to be thought, because it was considered not true by the wise men of many civilizations before our own. In short, the statement 'the computer does not impose' holds before us a view of the world with neutral instruments on one side and human autonomy on the other. But it is just that view of the world that needs to be thought if we are concerned with 'beyond industrial growth.'

To go further: how widely are we being asked to take the word 'ways' in the assertion that 'the computer does not impose the *ways*'? Even if the purposes for which the computer's capabilities should be used are determined outside itself, are not these capabilities determinative of the ways it can be used? To continue the illustration from the structures of learning and training which are part of all advanced technological societies: in Ontario there are cards on which local school authorities can assess children as to their intellectual 'skills' and 'behaviour.' This information is retained by computers. It may be granted that such computer cards add little to the homogenizing vision of learning inculcated into the structure by such means as, for example, centrally controlled teacher training. It may also be granted that, as computers and their use are more sophisticatedly developed, the 'information' stored therein will increasingly take account of differences. Nevertheless it is clear that the 'ways' that computers can be used for storing 'information' can only be ways that increase the tempo of the homogenizing process in society. Abstracting facts so that they may be stored as 'information' is achieved by classification, and it is the very nature of any classifying to homogenize what may be heterogeneous. Where classification rules, identities and differences can only appear in its terms. The capabilities of any computer do not allow it to be used neutrally towards the facts of heterogeneity. Moreover, classification by large institutions through investment-heavy machines is obviously not carried out because of the pure desire to know but because of convenience of organization.

It is not my purpose at this point to discuss the complex issues of good and evil involved in the modern movement towards homogeneity, or to discuss heterogeneity in its profoundest past form, autochthony. This would require a long discussion of Heidegger's thought. He, the greatest contemporary thinker of technique, seems to be claiming that beyond the homelessness of the present, human beings are now called to a new way of being at home which has passed through the most extreme homelessness. What is at issue here is simply that the statement about computers tends to hide the fact that their very capabilities entail that the ways they can be used are never neutral. They can only be used in homogenizing ways. And because this tends to be hidden in the statement, the question about the goodness of homogenization is excluded from the thinking of what it could be to be beyond industrial growth.

To illustrate the matter from another area of technical change: Canadians wanted the most efficient car for geographic circumstances almost similar to those in the country which had first developed a car usable by many. Our desire for and use of such cars has been a central cause of our political integration and social homogenization with the people of the imperial heartland. This was not only because of the vast imperial organizations necessary for building and keeping in motion such cars, and the direct and indirect political influence of such organizations, but also because the society with such vehicles tends to become like every other society with the same. Fifty years ago men might have said 'the automobile does not impose on us the ways it should be used.' This would have been a deluding representation of the automobile. In fact, human beings may still be able to control the ways that cars are used by preventing, for example, their pollution of the atmosphere or their freeways from destroying the centre of our cities. Indeed, in Canada, we may be able to deal better with such questions, as the history of the Spadina expressway may show, although the history of transportation in Montreal speaks in the other direction. Moreover, in the light of the huge crisis presented to westerners by the awakening of the Arabs to modernity, we may even be forced to pass beyond the private automobile as the chief means of mobility. Be that as it may, this cannot allow us to represent the automobile to ourselves as a neutral instrument. In so doing we have abstracted the productive functions of General Motors or Standard Oil from their political and social functions, just as their public relations would want. Moreover, we would have abstracted the automobile from the relations between such corporations and the public and private corporations of other centres of empire. Can one speak about 'values' and 'ideals' as if unaware of what reliable economists tell us: if the present rate of growth of IBM is extrapolated, that corporation will in twenty-five years be a larger economic unit than the economy of any presently constituted state, including that of its homeland?

Because of the suffered injustices in both the eastern and western societies, many educated people see the cutting issue to be decided as centring around whether technical advance is to be directed under capitalist or socialist control. What matters is whether the computer is used in ways which are capitalist or socialist. Some of the best of the young in the west are held by Marxism in revolt against our society, while it seems that some of the best in eastern Europe are liberals in reaction against their society. Despite all the abuses committed in the name of Marxism in eastern societies, this way of thought has remained a powerful minority influence in the west, just because it seems to point to a more equitable development of technical society than is possible under state capitalism. Also Marxism, as a system of thought, is more successful than the liberal ideologies of the west in placing technique within a corporate framework of purpose beyond the individual. At any stage of capitalism the interests of all are contractually subordinated to the interests of some. Marxism has been the chief source of a continuing critique of the facts that our social purposes are determined by private interests and that science is often harnessed to those purposes by calling it 'value-free.' On the other side, the liberal ideologists have asserted that our structures lead to a profounder liberation than is possible under Marxist socialism. This assertion is based not only on the negative criticism that communism is inevitably inhibited into a rancorous and cruel statism, but also on the positive judgment that capitalist freedom better opens the way to the development of technical science. The claims of the western empire that their system better liberates technology are neither insincere nor unsubstantiated. The present desire of Russia for American computers surely illustrates that.

However, amidst the passionate ideologies, it is well to remember what Marxism and American liberalism (two western-produced beliefs) hold in common. They both believe that the good progress of the race is in the direction of the universal society of free and equal human beings, that is towards the universal and homogeneous state. They both assert that the technology, which comes out of the same account of reason, is the necessary and good means to that end. In saying this I do not mean to encourage any of that nonsense about 'the end of ideology,' which was put about by a shallow American sociologist a decade ago. Those who think that the crucial question about technological societies is whether they develop under Marxist or liberal 'ideals' are given in that thought a source of responsibility for our present situation. (Who cannot prefer such ardent people to the vast numbers of the detached who currently retreat into a banal privacy?) Nevertheless, because of their belief in these ideologies, they are likely to forget that both sides of the controversy share assumptions which are more fundamental than that which divides them. At the immediate and flaming surface is their common assumption concerning the dependence of the achievement of a better society in the future upon the mastery of the human and the non-human by technological science. And that assumption comes forth from a series of deeper assumptions concerning what is. For example, it is assumed there is something we call 'history' over against 'nature,' and that it is in that 'history' that human beings have acquired their 'rationality.' To put it in the pedantic language of scholarship about the history of western thought: both Marxism and liberalism are penetrated in their ultimate assumptions by the thoughts of Rousseau; and in his thought about the origins of human beings the concept of reason as historical makes its extraordinary public arrival.

What calls out for recognition here is that the same apprehension of what it is to be 'reasonable' leads men to build computers and to conceive the universal and homogeneous society as the highest political goal. The ways such machines can be used must be at one with certain conceptions of political purposes, because the same kind of 'reasoning' made the machines and formulated the purposes. To put the matter extremely simply: the modern 'physical' sciences and the modern 'political' sciences have developed in mutual interpenetration, and we can only begin to understand that interpenetration in terms of some common source from which both forms of science found their sustenance. Indeed to think 'reasonably' about the modern account of reason is of such difficulty because that account has structured our very thinking in the last centuries. For this reason scholars are impotent in the understanding of it because they are trying to understand that which is the very form of how they understand. The very idea that 'reason' is that reason which allows us to conquer objective human and non-human nature controls our thinking about everything.

It cannot be my purpose here to describe the laying of the foundations of that interpenetration of the physical and moral sciences which is at the heart of western 'history' and now of world destiny. Such a mapping of those foundations would require detailed exposition of our past: what was made and thought and done by the inventors, the scientists, the philosophers, the theologians, the artists, the reformers, the politicians. Scholarship is very different from thought, although it often pretends to be the same. But good scholarship can be a support for thought, in the same way that good doctors can be a support for health. Suffice it to say here that the root of modern history lies in a particular experience of 'reason,' and the interpenetration of the human and non-human sciences that grew from that root. It is an occurrence which has not yet been understood. Nevertheless it is an event the significance of which for good or evil must now be attempted to be thought. The statement: 'the computer does not impose on us *the ways* it should be used' hides that interpenetration. To repeat, it simply presents us with neutral instruments which we in our freedom can shape to our 'values' and 'ideals.' But the very conceptions 'values' and 'ideals' come from the same form of reasoning which built the computers. 'Computers' and 'values' both come forth from that stance which summoned the world before it to show its reasons and bestowed 'values' on the world. Those 'values' are supposed to be the creations of human beings and have, linguistically, taken the place of the traditional 'good,' which was not created but recognized. In short, computers do not present us with neutral means for building any kind of society. All their alternative ways lead us towards the universal and homogeneous state. Our use of them is exercised within that mysterious modern participation in what we call 'reason.' Participation in that particular conception of reason is the strangest of all our experiences, and the most difficult to think in its origins.

To go further: because computers are produced from modern reasoning, the strongest ambiguity in the statement, 'the computer does not impose on us the ways it *should* be used,' is that our novelty is presented to us as if human beings 'should' use these machines for certain purposes and not for others. But what does the word 'should' mean in advanced technological societies? Is it not of the essence of our novelty that 'shouldness,' as it was once affirmed, can no longer hold us in its claiming?

'Should' was originally the past tense of 'shall.' It is still sometimes used in a conditional sense to express greater uncertainty about the future than the use of 'shall': ('I shall get a raise this year' is more certain than 'I should get a raise this year.' The same is in that wonderful colloquialism from the home of our language: 'I shouldn't wonder.') 'Should' has gradually taken over the sense of 'owing' from 'shall.' (In its origins 'owing' was given in the word 'shall' when used as a transitive verb.) In the sentence 'the computer does not impose on us the ways it *should* be used' we are speaking about human actions which express 'owing.' If the statement about computers were in positive form 'the computer *does* impose on us the ways it should be used,' the debt would probably be understood as from human beings to the machine. We can say of a good car that we owe it to the car to lubricate it properly or not to ride the clutch. We would mean it in the same sense that we owe it to ourselves to try to avoid contradicting ourselves, if we wish to think out some matter clearly. If we want the car to do what it is fitted for – which is, in the traditional usage, its good – then we must look after it. But the 'should' in the statement about the computer is clearly not being used about what is owed from men to the machine. What is then the nature of the debt there spoken? To what or to whom do human beings owe it? Is that debt conditional? For example, if men 'should' use computers only in ways that are compatible with constitutional government and never as instruments of tyranny, to what or to whom is this required support of constitutional government owed? To ourselves? to other human beings? to evolution? to nature? to 'history'? to reasonableness? to God?

There have been many descriptions of our time as essentially characterized by a darkening or even disappearance of any conception of good. These have often been made by those who are dismayed by the uncertainty of our era and find solace from the suffering of that dismay in nostalgia for some other era. Indeed as human beings have come to believe that their affirmations of goodness are not justified by reason or nature, history, or God, the effect upon many has been what some have called 'nihilism.' This belief has had wide political significance because it has become possible for many through mass literacy. Mass training has produced in North America that intensely vulgar phenomenon, popular wised-up-ness. I include within mass training the present university system. Nevertheless, it is incorrect to characterize the modern west as a society of nihilism, that is, as if people had no sense of what is good. If we used the word 'good' in its most general modern sense to stand for that which we approve, and 'bad' for that which we deplore, it is evident that the majority of modern people give their shared approval to certain forms of life. Can we not say that for most 'freedom' to do what they want in such realms as sexuality is an evident good? Most modern people consider good those political leaders who combine seeming resolution with evident charm. The very influence of ideologies in our era, whether Marxism, American liberalism, or National Socialism, has surely not been a mark of nihilism, but rather a mark of how much human beings wanted the evident goods that were put before them evidently.

Therefore, it is deluding if we characterize our novel modern situation as nihilistic. But at the same time we have to be aware that some great change has taken place. To characterize that change, it is best to state that it has fallen to the lot of people who are truly modern to apprehend goodness in a different way from all previous societies. 'Goodness' is now apprehended in a way which excludes from it all 'owingness.' To generalize this as clearly as I am able: the traditional western view of goodness is that which meets us with an excluding claim and persuades us that in obedience to that claim we will find what we are fitted for. The modern view of goodness is that which is advantageous to our creating richness of life (or, if you like, the popular modern propagandists' 'quality of life').

What is true of the modern conception of goodness (which appears in advanced technological societies and which distinguishes it from older conceptions of goodness) is that it does not include the assertion of an owed claim which is intrinsic to our desiring. Owing is always provisory upon what we desire to create. Obviously we come upon the claims of others and our creating may perforce be limited particularly by the state, because of what is currently permitted to be done to others. However such claims, whether within states or internationally, are seen as contractual, that is provisional. This exclusion of non-provisory owing from our interpretation of desire means that what is summoned up by the word 'should' is no longer what was summoned up among our ancestors. Its evocation always includes an 'if.' Moreover, the arrival in the world of this changed interpretation of goodness is interrelated to the arrival of technological civilization. The liberation of human desiring from any supposed excluding claim, so that it is believed that we freely create values, is a face of the same liberation in which men overcame chance by technology – the liberty to make happen what we want to make happen.

'The computer does not impose on us the ways it *should* be used' asserts the very essence of the modern view (human ability freely to determine what happens) and then puts that freedom in the service of the very 'should' which that same modern novelty has denied. The resolute mastery to which we are summoned in 'does not impose' is the very source of difficulty in apprehending goodness as 'should.' Therefore, the 'should' in the statement has only a masquerading resonance when it is asked to provide positive moral content to the actions we are summoned to concerning computers. It is a word carried over from the past to be used in a present which is only ours because the assumptions of that past were criticized out of public existence. The statement therefore cushions us from the full impact of the novelties it asks us to consider. It pads us against wondering about the disappearance of 'should' in its ancient resonance, and what this disappearance may portend for the future.

Statements such as this are increasingly common in the liberal world because we feel the need to buttress the morality of our managers in their daily decisions.

Indeed, the more it becomes possible to conceive that we might not be able to control the immensity of the apparatus and the constantly changing emergencies it presents us with, the more intense become the calls for moral 'values' and 'ideals.' Technological society is presented to us as a set of neutral means, something outside ourselves, and human beings are presented as in touch with some constant, from out of which constancy they are called upon to deal with the new external crises. But obviously all that is given us in the technological sciences denies that constancy, that eternality. What happens is that constancy is appealed to in practical life and denied in intellectual life. In such a situation the language of eternality is gradually removed from all serious public realms, because it is made completely unresonant by what dominates the public world. The residual and unresonant constant appealed to in the sentence about the computer is the word 'should.' But the intellectual life which allowed the coming to be of computers has also made 'should' almost unthinkable.

I have discussed this sentence at great length to show that when we look at our present situation as if we in our freedom were called upon to impose 'values' and 'ideals' on technological situations seen as 'objective' to us, we are not beyond industrial growth, but within that which brought industrial growth to be. 'Values' and 'ideals,' 'persons' and 'the creating of history' are at their very heart the technological speaking. Let me concentrate my essential point in a criticism of a recent writing by Professor C. B. Macpherson. In his *Democratic Theory*, an early section is entitled 'The race between ontology and technology.' It is just such words that I am trying to show as deluding. Macpherson identifies ontologies with 'views of the essence of man,' and writes of 'a fateful race between ontological change and technological change.' One might ask: is not technological change an aspect of what is, and therefore not something other than ontological change? But what is above all misleading in such words is that they obscure the fact that every act of scientific discovery or application comes forth from an ontology which so engrosses us that it can well be called our western destiny. Technology is not something over against ontology; it is the ontology of the age. It is for us an almost inescapable destiny. The great question is not then 'the race between technology and ontology,' but what is the ontology which is declared in technology? What could it be to be 'beyond' it, and would it be good to be 'beyond' it?

The foregoing has not been stated for the sake of increasing the sense of human impotence. Aesthetic pessimism is a form of self-indulgence to which protected academics are particularly prone. In so far as one is aware that one is prone to such sick pessimism, it should be dealt with in privacy and not presented publicly. It always matters what we do. Moreover, at a much deeper level, authentic despair is a human possibility and a very great evil. Therefore it must be prepared for. Our first obligation is to seek acquaintance with joy so that any arrival of despair does not carry us into madness. The complete absence of joy is madness. However, the stating of the facts in any given situation has nothing to do with despair, but only with the possible destruction of inadequate sources of hope – the destruction of which is a necessary part of all our lives.

Rather my purpose is to state the profundity with which technological civilization enfolds us as our destiny. Coming to meet us out of the very substance of our past, that destiny has now become, not only our own, but that of the species as a whole. Moreover, this destiny is not alone concerned with such obvious externals that we can blow ourselves up or ameliorate diabetes or have widespread freedom from labour or watch our distant wars on television. It is a destiny which presents us with what we think of the whole, with what we think is good, with what we think good is, with how we conceive sanity and madness, beauty and ugliness. It is a destiny which enfolds us in our most immediate experiences: what we perceive when we encounter a bird or a tree, a child or a road. It equally enfolds us in less tangible apperceptions such as temporality. My cruder purpose is to make clear that that destiny is not a situation like picking and choosing in a supermarket; rather, it is like a package deal.

When we, as western people, put to ourselves the question of what can lie 'beyond industrial growth,' we are liable to be asking it as a problem within the package which is that destiny. It is taken as a problem of the same order as that which we are currently meeting because of our dependence on oil and the Arab awakening. To say this is not to belittle such problems or to seem to stand in proud aloofness from them. They have to be met and will require great wisdom – indeed greater wisdom than has characterized our English-speaking rulers since 1914.

However, even at the immediate level of the pragmatic, the questioning in 'beyond industrial growth' begins to reveal the universal which is spoken in technology. We move into the tightening circle in which more technological science is called for to meet the problems which technological science has produced. In that tightening circle, the overcoming of chance is less and less something outside us, but becomes more and more the overcoming of chance in our own species, in our very own selves. Every new appeal for a more exact cybernetics means, in fact, forceful new means of mastery over the most intimate aspects of the lives of masses of people. Particularly among some of those who are the patients of that mastery and among those who keep some hesitation about their part in enforcing it, questioning cannot be wholly repressed. For example, will it be possible to hide entirely what is being spoken universally about our own species in the massive programs of foetuscide which characterize modern societies? Will it be possible to hide what is being spoken universally in the advances in reproductive biology and behavioural psychology, as those advances become part of our everyday lives? Moreover, when what is spoken there universally is listened to, will it be able to be accepted as including in its universality the hunger and thirst for justice?

For thinkers, the universal in 'beyond industrial growth' must appear as the package deal becomes increasingly explicit. With that explicitness inevitably comes the central theoretical question of this era. Can our thinking be satisfied with the historicist universal? If the universal appearing as historicism can be known as only a masquerading of the universal, then it will be possible to ask the following question: in all that has been practised and thought and made by western human beings in their dedication to the overcoming of chance, what has there been of good? What has perhaps been found? What has perhaps been lost? What have these possible losings and findings to do with what we can know of the trans-historical whole?

It looks very likely that amidst the pressing calls for cybernetic organization in our immediate future, there will be little social patience for those who think about these questions. Thinkers will be accused of vagueness and uncertainty, impracticality and self-indulgence in times of crisis. For example, it is clear that the great intellectual achievement of modernity is its physics, and that the scientific community which ultimately feeds on that achievement is the most intellectually influential in our midst. Yet in its pride, that community is, with rare exceptions, contemptuous and impatient of any thought which is 'beyond' solutions. Historicist scholarship is tolerated because it is unlikely to pass over into thought. Therefore, I would predict that those who want to think will have to develop a more than usual irony to protect themselves from this impatience.

In the face of the complexity, immensity, and uncertainty of that which calls to be questioned, it may, indeed, seem that thinkers are impotent as aids to the inescapable immediacies of the public realm. The originating tradition concerning rationality in the west was that it had something to do with happiness and therefore something to do with throwing light upon the awful responsibilities of time. In the ambiguous heart of Plato's dialogues, philosophy included political philosophy. This relation to practice may seem to have been lost when thinkers are called to wander in the chasms which have been opened up by education for the overcoming of chance. It may seem that, when thought wanders in these chasms, it becomes useless to the public realm. Yet the darkness which envelops the western world because of its long dedication to the overcoming of chance is just a fact. Thinkers who deny the fact of that darkness are no help in illuminating a finely tempered practice for the public realm. The job of thought at our time is to bring into the light that darkness as darkness. If thinkers are turned away from this by becoming tamed confederates in the solution of some particular problem, they have turned away from the occupation they are called to. The consequent division between thought and practice is therefore even greater than at most times and places. That division is a price that has to be paid by people given over primarily either to practice or to thought, because of the false unity between thought and practice which has dominated our civilization so long in its dedication to the overcoming of chance. That false unity presses on us in the two leading ideologies of our age – Marxism and American liberalism – in both of which thought has been made almost to disappear as it was perverted into a kind of practice.

Those of us who are Christians have been told that there is something 'beyond' both thought and practice. Both are means or ways. In their current public division from each other, the memory of their joint insufficiency will be helpful to both. What is also necessary for both types of life is a continuing dissatisfaction with the fact that the darkness of our era leads to such a division between them. In this dissatisfaction lies the hope of taking a first step: to bring the darkness into light as darkness.

CONTRIBUTORS

CLAUDE CASTONGUAY is a former Minister of Health, Family and Social Welfare in the Quebec government. He is now an actuary and consultant.

GEORGE GRANT is Professor of Religion at McMaster University.

A.W. JOHNSON is a former Deputy Minister of Welfare in Ottawa and is now President of the Canadian Broadcasting Corporation.

MAURICE LAMONTAGNE was formerly Secretary of State in the federal government and is now a Senator.

VIVIAN RAKOFF is Professor of Psychiatric Education at the University of Toronto.

CHARLES TAYLOR is a Professor of Political Science and Philosophy at McGill University.

ABRAHAM ROTSTEIN is a Senior Fellow of Massey College and a member of the Department of Political Economy at the University of Toronto.